GW00385044

Happiness!
Is It Simply A Mindset Shift?

Also by Shalini Bhalla-Lucas

Always With You
A true story of love, loss… and hope

Online Dating @ 40
The Nobheads, Nutjobs & Nice Guys

Praise for *Always With You*:

*"An evocative and poignantly written memoir.
Shalini Bhalla-Lucas has extensively researched the issues which
have affected and shaped her life such as religion, meditation, mental
health illness and bereavement."*

*"Shalini writes with such heartfelt honesty, and such warmth.
You couldn't fail to be touched by this book."*

"Beautiful, moving and thought-provoking."

"A complete inspiration."

Praise for *Online Dating @ 40*

*"This is a searingly honest and very funny (short) book that I am
sure many women who find themselves navigating the delights of
online dating will really relate to!"*

*"This book is funny, insightful, toe-curling, and at times raw. It
brilliantly illuminates one person's highs and lows of online dating."*

Happiness!
Is It Simply A Mindset Shift?

By Shalini Bhalla-Lucas

The right of Shalini Bhalla (Shalini Bhalla-Lucas)
to be identified as author of this work has been
asserted by the author in accordance with the
Copyright, Designs and Patents Act 1988

Copyright © 2020 Shalini Bhalla (Shalini Bhalla-Lucas)

All rights reserved. No part of this publication may be
reproduced, distributed, or transmitted in any form or by any
means, including photocopying, recording, or other electronic
or mechanical methods, without the prior written permission
of the publisher, except in the case of brief quotations
embodied in critical reviews and certain other noncommercial
uses permitted by copyright law. For permission requests,
write to the publisher at the address below.

Published by Just Jhoom! Ltd
PO Box 142, Cranleigh, Surrey, GU6 8ZX
info@justjhoom.co.uk
www.justjhoom.co.uk

Cover Design: Angela Basker
Author and Cover Photographs: Sian Tyrrell

ISBN: 9798623258281

*Please note that the meditations and exercises contained in this book may not be suitable for
everyone. If you are suffering from a mental health illness, or are unsure of the suitability of some
of the meditations, please consult a healthcare professional before embarking on this or any other
wellbeing programme. This book is not a substitute for medical or psychotherapeutic advice.
Pregnant women and people with high blood pressure should be especially careful when doing
some of the high energy meditations. The publisher, Just Jhoom! Ltd, or the author, Shalini Bhalla
(Shalini Bhalla-Lucas), make no representations or warranties with respect to the accuracy,
completeness, fitness for a particular purpose or currency of the contents of this book and exclude
all liability to the extent permitted by law for any errors or omissions in this book and for any loss,
damage or expense (direct or indirect) suffered by anyone relying on any information contained in
this book.*

For Dr Shivani Bhalla.

My sister, my inspiration, my hero.

Be happy. Always.

For Jeremy.

Who watches over me and gives me his blessing
as I create happiness in my life.
I carry you in my heart – always.

Kyonki yeh rishta roohani hain;
kyonki yeh rishta janum ki hai.
I love you – and I know you are always with me.

Ever yours. Ever mine. Ever ours.

Table of Contents

"There is no path to happiness.
Happiness is the path."
Shakyamuni Buddha[1]

"Happiness depends upon ourselves."
Aristotle[2]

Foreword

What an honour to be asked to write the foreword for this thought-provoking and insightful book.

Shalini Bhalla-Lucas was savaged by grief but has found the strength to turn it into a life-affirming experience. Her journey of discovery has been painful but through determination and courage she has been able to shine a light on what really matters in life – happiness.

In this deeply personal and heart-warming book, Shalini talks about her own tragedy and journey to define and create happiness. Her simple belief that happiness can be cultivated in our lives even when we are faced with untold pain, adversity and challenges, and her determination to share her journey, is moving. Happiness is that elusive mindset that everyone wants but few know how to attain.

The key message, in the words of the Dalai Lama, is that *"Happiness is not something ready-made, it comes from your actions"*. We can, through our conscious effort find wisdom, harmony, strength and happiness. There is purpose in our lives and often the purpose is hidden. Discovering it through mindfulness, gratitude, compassion, relationships and learning leads to happiness.

This book provides numerous tools and techniques to incorporate happiness into our lives. To align the mind, body and spirit in a way that makes for a life filled with joy and meaning.

This is an uplifting book written with warmth and openness, and packed with deep insights. A book that will undoubtedly enrich the lives of all its readers and help them on their journey of discovery.

Pinky Lilani CBE DL

Introduction

The Dalai Lama[3] was once asked, "What is the meaning of life?" He answered immediately. "The meaning of life is *happiness*." He went on to say, "Hard question is not, 'What is meaning of life?' That is easy question to answer! No, hard question is what *makes* happiness. Money? Big house? Accomplishment? Friends? Or..." And then he paused. "Compassion and good heart? This is the question all human beings must try to answer: *What makes true happiness*?"

And it is a question I have wrestled with for years.

Namaste. I'm Shalini Bhalla-Lucas and in July 2016 my beautiful, kind husband Jeremy died from a rare form of renal cancer. It was the most devastating thing to have happened to me in my life. Before he died, I had other challenging life experiences such as family estrangement, failure at work, struggles with depression and anxiety – but nothing prepared me for the grief that I would feel following his death.

Grief is so universal and yet so very personal. It is a merciless master. It holds you in a vice-like grip, pulling you down to the very depths of despair. And in those depths of despair I didn't think I would ever be happy again. But, as time passes, the grip of grief does loosen. I think of the pain that grief causes as a large stone that you carry. At first the stone is heavy and has very jagged edges. Those jagged edges keep piercing you in your heart causing unbearable pain. But, over time, those jagged edges smooth away and you are left with a dull, heavy ache. That ache, that heaviness, never quite goes away. And nor should it. Because that ache – which is sometimes very strong, and sometimes weak, but always there – reminds you that you loved this person you have lost and that you were once loved by them. It reminds you that your love is eternal.

As my grief slowly began to lift, I realised that I wanted to move forward with my life but I didn't know how. I knew I would never move on from my husband, but I was still young – only in my 40s. I wanted to live my life and I knew that my husband would want that for me too - I had no doubt about that.

My father died 18 months after Jeremy passed away and it was a huge turning point for me. I had seen these two men fight to live – but cancer got them in the end.

Jeremy had made sure that I would be financially secure when he died. In the 19 years that we had been together, he had also encouraged and supported me to be an independent, successful career woman. So, I had that to fall back on. My father had given me a great childhood and superb education which enabled me to be independent, strong and empowered. So surely, if they couldn't live then I could – for them and for myself.

But moving forward wasn't so easy because I didn't know *how* to move forward. You see, I had forgotten what happiness was. I had forgotten *how* to be happy.

So, when things seem so very difficult and moving forward seems almost impossible, how do we do it? Where do we get not only the strength to face each day, but to face it with optimism, compassion and the will to live life fully and to the best of our ability? And most importantly, how do we find happiness in our daily lives?

I was fortunate to have seen the Dalai Lama speak in London in 2015, and I was reminded of what he said about the meaning of life. I was struck by his message of compassion, tolerance and happiness. I needed to learn more. And what I learnt blew my mind. I share some of my findings here in this book.

Perhaps what struck me most in my search for happiness is that you don't find happiness... you create it! Yes, happiness can be cultivated. We can create happiness in our lives even when faced with untold pain, adversity and challenges.

So, how did I cultivate happiness, compassion and resilience in my life?

I did it by adopting 10 simple but hugely effective techniques which I am so eager and excited to share with you.

These techniques, some of which are daily rituals, have changed my life. They are not a quick fix, but rather a way of life, and by embodying them I have been able to face each day on an even keel.

I believe there are three elements to each of us – mind, body and spirit. As we are holistic beings, to achieve happiness we need to ensure all our three elements are aligned. The techniques that I will share with you, focus on all three elements and help ensure your mind, body and spirit work in harmony.

I present these 10 techniques in Part 2 of this book with some free online resources to accompany them on my website.

Before you start adopting these techniques, I want to share a wonderful Samburu proverb[4]:

Keata Nkishon Larin
Life Consists of Seasons

Life is not one long season; one smooth journey. Rather, it is a series of chopping and changing times, both happy and sad, serene and tumultuous. Each of these seasons brings with it both good and bad experiences, and through these experiences we learn the lessons we need in this lifetime. And so, as the seasons change, so do we. And, if we can face these seasons with the resilience and strength of mind, body and spirit, then we have a much better chance of showing up when it's necessary, speaking our truth when we once thought we couldn't and standing in our power to live this one precious gift of life in the best possible way.

After all, this is what life is about!
We fall, we rise; we fail, we learn; we cry, we laugh; we love, we grow; we live.

Surely, if by changing our mindset we can decide to live a happier life, a more joyful life, then isn't it worth a try?

I'm grateful for this opportunity to share these techniques with you through this book. I would love to hear from you. Please connect with me on Facebook/Twitter/Instagram – @justjhoom

After all, human connection and building relationships is a key to happiness.

So, let's start today. Me and you.

With much love and gratitude.

Namaste.

Shalini Bhalla-Lucas
Nanyuki, Kenya, 2020

Part 1

Happiness

"Happiness is experiences of pleasure and purpose over time."
Paul Dolan[5]

Chapter 1
Happiness as a Science

Happiness is a science. It has been studied as such since the 1980s and so much has been written about it.

I am not going to go into the deep science of happiness here. There are many books that do that and will do it much better than me. I have listed some of my favourites in the Further Reading section at the back of this book.

But I do want to share with you the key messages that I have taken away and that have enabled me to be happy.

Research shows that there are three elements to our happiness. The first element, which accounts for around 50 per cent of our happiness, is our genetic makeup. And this genetic makeup determines our proclivity to happiness. It is our genetic set point so we can't really change it but we can work with it.

The second element accounts for 10 per cent of our happiness. Now, remember that... 10 per cent. So, what is this 10 per cent? It is social status, money, the job we do, where we live and our age. Yes –

surprisingly this accounts for *only* 10 per cent. And yet these extrinsic goals of money, image and status are, without doubt, seen by most people in our society, as the most significant factors in our quest for happiness. Interestingly enough, once your basic needs are met, more money doesn't necessarily mean more happiness. And focusing on these things can lead to depression, anxiety, sadness and overall less satisfaction.

This really is food for thought and when I considered it carefully, I realised that for much of my adult life I had focused on these extrinsic goals, perhaps contributing to my anxiety and depression. I put a lot of emphasis on being successful in my career, sometimes to the detriment of relationships and friendships. I was motivated by making money, often working so hard that it affected my physical and mental health. And I was overly concerned by what people thought of me, leading to anxiety, 'imposter syndrome' and a feeling that I was just not good enough.

So, what about the remaining 40 per cent? This is where it gets exciting. This 40 per cent is where we can really influence our sense of happiness. These are the intentional behaviours or activities we can engage in to make us happier. It is the intrinsic goals such as personal growth, positive relationships and the desire to help others that account for this 40 per cent.

In a nutshell, it is the difference between the 10 per cent of fleeting pleasure and 40 per cent of deep contentment.

When my reading and research led to this understanding about happiness, it made so much sense. The idea that I could nurture a long-lasting, deep contentment instead of the transient, ephemeral pleasure that I had been used to was a revelation. There was just one problem. *I didn't know how to do this.*

I decided to start with what I knew. So, I began to take all the skills and knowledge I had acquired over the years as a dance and mindfulness teacher, and as a writer, and I started developing and adopting certain techniques and daily rituals into my life in the hope that I would create and foster lasting happiness.

Now this is not to say that on some days I don't feel sad or angry or fearful. That would be unrealistic. To know happiness, you need to know sadness. To know pleasure, you must know pain. That's how your brain works – it understands contrasts.

But those feelings of sadness, anger and fear do not last long. This is because one of the key ingredients to happiness is the ability to recover from adversity more quickly. It's about showing an appropriate response to hardships in your life and then coming back to your genetic set point quickly. This is called 'resilience'.

Resilience, as defined by the *Concise Oxford Dictionary*[6], is *"readily recovering from shock, depression, etc.; buoyant"*.

Some people are born with an inner resilience, but most of us will learn it through the trials and tribulations that we face in our daily lives.

You can either stay down after you have been knocked down by life's challenges, or after each fall you can choose to get back up, stronger and more resilient to face the next challenge life throws you.

Being happy is a decision we make, a brave one, in the face of, and as a response to, all life's challenges.

The choice is yours.

Chapter 2
The Wolves in Our Hearts

There is a wonderful Native American parable about the two wolves that live in all our hearts. One wolf is the Wolf of Love and the other is the Wolf of Hate.

In each one of us there is a fight between the two wolves. The Wolf of Hate is evil and fed by fear, anger, greed, guilt and ego. The Wolf of Love is good and it is fed by tolerance, peace, compassion, truth and humility.

So, which wolf will win the fight? Quite simply, the one you feed.

We often find that we are feeding the Wolf of Hate subconsciously. Feelings of fear and guilt often arise without us even realising or noticing them. And this is something we have to address.

We have to learn to feed the Wolf of Love and not in a whimsical way, but in a meaningful, sustainable and practical way.

The nature of our thoughts can actually change the

neural structure of our brain. Our mind can change our brain for the better.

But it is not easy. What we need to remember is that our brains are still stuck in the stone age. Not good news! It means that our brains have evolved towards a negative bias. This was useful when we were faced with fight or flight situations and our survival relied on us predicting when danger may arise. Unfortunately, because our brains haven't really evolved that much, we still see each day as a survival experience.

So, the negative effect of a setback impacts us twice as strongly as the positive effect of a success. The brain is like a magnet for negative experiences. Once a negative experience is in the brain it just sticks, whereas a positive experience flows through the brain much quicker. It's more transient.

This is why we worry so much. We focus on the negative aspects and the negative thoughts that come into our mind a lot more than focusing on the positives.

And we often do this subconsciously. Our brains go into autopilot and we get trapped in a quagmire of negative thoughts which in turn feeds the Wolf of Hate inside us.

The ABC Model of Emotions[7] explains this well.

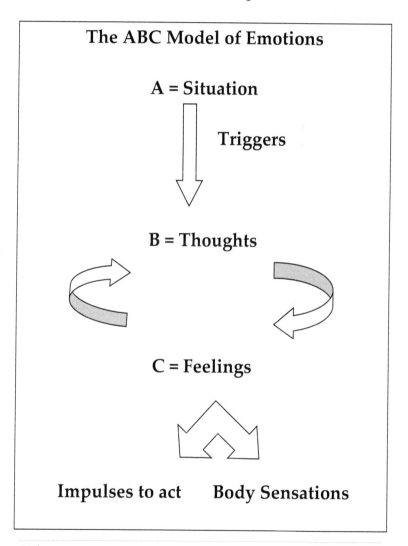

The premise of the model is that two people watching the exact same scenario unfold could perceive it very differently based on their life experiences, preconceptions, assumptions and natural/biological bias.

Your perception of the situation affects your feelings and emotions and these determine your thoughts. That emotional response triggers more thoughts and more emotions in a cyclical process, which then triggers off your response, resulting in an impulsive, physiological reaction.

So, for example, if you were to see a friend across the street, and you waved to them and they didn't wave back your immediate thought could be, "*Why didn't she wave back? Did I do something to offend her? Is she angry with me?*" These thoughts lead to your emotional response such as fear that you have offended your friend. Your body reacts with your heart beating faster, a feeling of anxiety in your chest. It could then lead to you thinking, "*Well that's just not on. Who does she think she is that she can ignore me like that?*" This leads to feelings of anger and you might get hot in the face. Or, it could lead to feelings of sadness, "*I'm sad I have hurt her. I really hope I don't lose a friend because of something I've done.*" You could feel heavy hearted.

Depending on your thoughts and emotions, your reaction could be that you decide to ignore your friend next time you see her, or perhaps you drop her a message later that day to see if everything is okay.

Of course, the reality could be that when you waved at your friend, she didn't actually see you waving at her. So, all the negative thoughts and emotions were triggered by your perception of the situation.

It is important to take charge of our brains to avoid this autopilot thinking. And this is where mindfulness and awareness come in. The brain is an organ but it can be likened to a muscle. In the same way you have to exercise to keep your body and muscles fit, you have to train your brain to be fit, training it like a muscle to be more aware of negative thoughts. Once we have trained our minds to be more aware of our thoughts, we start to lead more mindful lives, which then means we start nurturing the Wolf of Love inside us and therefore banish the Wolf of Hate.

So which wolf will win the battle inside your heart?

The choice is yours.

Chapter 3
Happiness and Positive Action

Often when we are faced by a challenge in life, our well-meaning friends and family will say, *"Don't worry. Everything will be fine. Just stay positive."*

But what does this mean? And is thinking positively enough?

I realised that cultivating lasting happiness was not just about positive thinking. It was about positive action. You see, happiness is a skill that we can all work on, but you can't just think yourself happy, you have to take positive actions to create that real, deep contentment we all so desire.

The Greek philosopher Socrates (469 – 399 BC) is perhaps one of the best advocates of this, believing that happiness can be obtained by human endeavour. He believed that you had to control your desires and find an inner state of tranquility that external factors could not affect.

Just reading about happiness is not enough. Just talking about happiness is not enough. Just thinking about happiness is not enough. You have to create and nurture happiness. You have to practise happiness. You have to create a physical, mental and spiritual state of stability that fosters happiness.

And this is what this book will help you do. Rather than dwell on the science of happiness it will give you the tools to create an equilibrium and a harmony in all three aspects of your life – your physical, mental and spiritual health – and so creating and nurturing deep contentment and joyfulness in your life. Read about my experiences. See what adversities I have gone through and then how I have worked on my mind, my body and my spirit to create a resilience that allows me to face all challenges that come my way.

This resilience has meant that each time I have fallen in the face of adversity, I haven't fallen as low or as hard as the last time. And each time I have risen to the challenge, I have risen faster and stronger. That old adage, *"what doesn't kill you makes you stronger"*, is so true.

But it is important to note that I don't just visit these techniques when I need them. Instead, I have embodied them in my life. I treat them as vital and intrinsic parts of daily survival, like the need to eat and sleep. And like everything, the more I practised, the more of a habit they became, the more natural they felt, and the more they became   embedded into my daily routine. This is what you must work towards.

Take each technique, learn it, apply it and embody it. Slowly you will notice that your mindset begins to change. And then, you will find that you are on this wonderful journey, this path to happiness.

Surely if changing your mindset gives you deep, inner happiness, it is worth putting the effort in.

The choice is yours.

Chapter 4
The 10 Techniques
that Make Me Happy

In Part 2 of this book, I share with you the 10 simple, yet hugely effective, techniques that I have adopted to cultivate happiness, compassion and resilience in my busy, daily life.

I suggest that you incorporate each step gradually. In my 10-step programme, you will introduce each step into your life at a weekly interval. Once you have got used to Step 1, you then introduce Step 2, and so on. By the end of 10 weeks, you will find that you have adopted the 10 steps seamlessly into your daily routine.

In every step you will find an introduction, meditations to learn and practise, and an action point to enable you to harness that step securely.

Remember that you have free guided online resources on my website.
To access these, please visit:
www.justjhoom.co.uk/happiness-free-resources/

Step 1
Living in the Now: Being Mindful

Mindfulness teaches you to live fully in the present moment. After all, that is all we have. The past is gone, and the future is unknown and beyond our control.

Step 2
Learn, Grow, Live: Keep Learning

I recently learnt to ride a motorbike – something I had always wanted to do but never had the courage to embark on. For me, this is what life is about. We learn, we grow, we live.

Step 3
The Power of Thought: Changing Your Mindset

Making the mental shift from what is wrong with our lives to what we want in our lives is often difficult. But this mental shift is an important one.

Step 4
The Joy of Gratitude: Being Grateful

It's well documented that people who express gratitude for what they have and what they experience, feel happier.

Step 5
Compassionate Me: Practising Compassion

Compassion is the act of being kind, showing

consideration and a spirit of generosity to all people (including yourself), animals and the environment.

Step 6
Nourish the Body: Getting Active
It's just wonderful that we are all so different and that we can turn to different activities - dance, yoga, sports, gardening, walking the dog, even housework - to keep us fit, healthy and happy.

Step 7
Power Your Presence: Be Seen, Be Heard
Being seen and being heard means having the confidence to be present, to be authentic and to have true connection with others.

Step 8
The   Art   of   Giving: Giving   to   Others
As a species, we are hardwired to be altruistic. That bond that we form with another when we do something for them with no expectation of a reward is reward in itself – and no monetary value can be put on that.

Step 9
Connection: Building Relationships
We must remember that authentic, real and personal connections we form with the people we encounter, even in brief encounters, can be truly magical.

Step 10
Nourishing the Body: Eating Well

I am quite fussy about what I eat. I am not keen on fast food, take-away meals and ready-made meals. I like my food to be freshly prepared with good, fresh, locally-sourced ingredients.

For a detailed explanation of each of the 10 steps, plus meditations and action points, read Part 2 of this book – Changing Your Mindset.

If at any time you feel really stuck on a step or find you have hit a brick wall, please write to me at happiness@justjhoom.co.uk and I will endeavour to help you through the process. And remember, at all times I am available on social media – Facebook, Twitter, Instagram – @justjhoom.

I look forward to hearing from you.

Happiness Journal

Writing a Happiness Journal is a good practice to adopt as you approach each step. At the end of each step, I will remind you to write your reflections about the meditations and action points in your journal. This doesn't have to be anything fancy. A notebook with or without lines – whatever works for you. I have numerous journals and they are all of varying sizes, styles and colours. The main thing about the journal is that it works for you, that you can carry it around easily, and that you can write in it whenever you want.

Take your time to write down how you felt about the meditation or exercise. As you do that, take note on how you feel – both about the act of writing itself and what you are writing about.

A good format to follow is:
1. Date and time of meditation or action point
2. Type of meditation
3. Any comments or observations

Your journal is private to you. Write how you feel; be honest, be open. Make sure that you keep the journal in a safe place away from prying eyes! If you wish, no one need ever read the journal except you.

Once in a while I read back to see what my feelings were about a particular meditation or happiness technique. I do this when I haven't practised a meditation for a while, and after reflecting on it, I see if anything has changed from then to the present moment.

Enjoy writing in your Happiness Journal; it is such a precious way to acknowledge how you are feeling in the present moment and what is working for you.

Part 2

Changing Your Mindset

"Happiness is not something readymade.
It comes from your own actions."
Dalai Lama[8]

Step 1
Living in the Now:
Being Mindful

Mindfulness is present moment awareness; deliberately paying attention to the here and now and the activity that you are engaged in. In this moment of pure awareness, you accept things for what they are, compassionately and without judgement.

> ### A Definition of Mindfulness
> *Mindfulness is the awareness that emerges through paying attention*
> *on purpose,*
> *in the present moment*
> *and*
> *non-judgmentally,*
> *to things as they are.*
> Williams, Teasdale, Segal, and Kabat-Zinn[9]

Mindfulness teaches you to live fully in the present moment. After all, that is all we have. The past is gone, and the future is unknown and beyond our control.

So much is now being written about mindfulness. And, it is being found in all spheres of life – from schools to hospitals, from the workplace to the community. Mindfulness has even been practised in the UK Parliament!

Although mindfulness is a non-religious practice, its roots can be found in Buddhism and it has been practised by Buddhists for centuries. Anyone from any faith or religion, from any background and of any age, can practise mindfulness and reap the benefits to live a more meaningful, peaceful and balanced life.

There are two main approaches to mindfulness developed in recent years and these are Mindfulness-Based Stress Reduction (MBSR) and Mindfulness-Based Cognitive Therapy (MBCT).

Mindfulness-Based Stress Reduction (MBSR)
This is probably the most well-proven stress reduction course and was developed by Jon Kabat-Zinn at the stress reduction clinic at the University of Massachusetts. Developed in the late 1970s, thousands of people have completed the eight-week MBSR programme with excellent results in responding to stress, pain, illness and the daily trials and tribulations of life.

Mindfulness-Based Cognitive Therapy (MBCT)

In the last decade or so, Professor Mark Williams, Dr John Teasdale and Professor Zindel Segal in the UK have developed MBCT for the treatment of depression, based on the MBSR programme. The MBCT programme aims to help people who have had depression stay well and not experience a relapse of the condition. MBCT introduces mindfulness skills that enable you to relate to any experience in a different way – a kind, compassionate and more mindful way.

Why Be Mindful?

Anxiety, stress, exhaustion, depression – these seem to be the norms of living in this fast-paced, frantic modern world.

In our search for happiness we continuously look to external forms of gratification and yet all the time the key to happiness – true happiness and a joyful existence – is deep within us.

Mindfulness and meditation are not religions. Rather they are a form of mental training. Using qualities like compassion and acceptance you learn to pay attention (and live) in the present moment. With a few minutes' practise every day you can begin to make life-long changes that will unlock the peace and contentment that is within you to overcome this relentless struggle that seems to epitomise our daily lives.

Seated meditation is the *formal* part of the mental training. You sit or lie and are guided, or self-guide, through meditations. The idea is that you take time out of your busy life and devote that time to meditating. Mindfulness activities, on the other hand, are the *informal* part of the mental training. This is where the exercises you practise are actually integrated into your daily life.

Both the formal and informal practices help to make your present moment awareness much stronger, more powerful. So, you live more fully in the present, enjoying the journey for what it is rather than living in the past or the future.

Benefits of Mindfulness
There are so many benefits to practising mindfulness and there are numerous studies to show this. Controlled experiments, evidence-based research and the testimonies of thousands of people are growing proof that mindfulness is not just a fad, but a genuine way to improve one's life.

Benefits include:

- Reduces stress
- Reduces depression (and relapse of depression)
- Combats anxiety
- Reduces chronic pain and boosting the immune system
- Encourages deeper sleep
- Increases overall happiness and wellbeing
- Boosts creativity
- Trains your brain!

Action Point

One-Minute Mindful Breathing Meditation

This really simple meditation can be done anywhere, anytime and is one of my favourite meditations because the effect that one minute has on me can be quite astounding. I often do this meditation when I am working and am being faced with a stressful situation or when I am over-tired and feeling a little grumpy. If faced with a difficult meeting or nerves just before an after-dinner speech, this is my go-to meditation. It calms me down, it focuses me, it centres me.

- You can do this seated or standing. Either way, make sure you are comfortable with your spine in neutral and your feet flat on the floor to ground you to the earth.
- Close your eyes if you feel comfortable to do so – if in a public place, just lower your gaze. Just sit or stand there for a moment.
- Now bring your attention to your breath. Exhale and inhale in your own time.
- Feel the different sensations as you breathe in and out – the breath on your upper lip, the rise and fall of your chest and stomach.
- Keep your attention on your breath.

- If you find your mind wandering, do not worry. Acknowledge that your mind has wandered, but don't judge yourself. Be kind to yourself. Gently bring your mind back to your breathing – and carry on.
- Whatever you are feeling – calm, angry, frustrated – just let it happen. Acknowledge your feelings – allowing them to be.
- And then, gently open your eyes.
- With practice, you can increase the time from one minute to two minutes to 10 minutes and so on. But, never underestimate that doing just one minute alone can also be truly powerful.

Adapted from Mindfulness – a Practical Guide to Finding Peace in a Frantic World, Williams and Pennman[10]

Counting the Breath Meditation

Seated meditations can be done sat on a chair or on the floor. Find a comfortable position that works for you and allows you to be grounded, stable and sitting with your back straight and dignified.

If you are seated on a chair make sure you are seated upright with your feet flat on the ground. You may need to sit forward in your chair. If you have any back pain then do support your back with cushions or the back of the chair. Place your hands lightly in your lap, palms facing up. Your spine should be in neutral, with your body aligned and sitting on your sitting bones. Ensure your neck and head are not jutting out but in alignment with the rest of your spine.

If seated on the floor use a mat. You can kneel, supporting your buttocks with a meditation stool or cushion or you can sit on some cushions to support your buttocks with your feet crossed in half lotus with your knees supported on the floor. Your hips need to be higher than your knees. Place your hands lightly in your lap, palms facing up. Ensure your neck and head are not jutting out but in alignment with the rest of your spine.

- Close your eyes if you feel comfortable to do so. Just sit with that for a moment.
- Now bring your attention to your breath. Exhale and inhale through your nose in your own time.
- Feel the different sensations as you breathe in and out – the breath on your upper lip, the rise and fall of your chest and stomach.
- Now, begin to mentally count your breath… In breath – one, out breath – two, in breath – three, out breath – four and so on until you reach 10. Then go back to counting from one.
- Keep your attention on your breath.

- If you find your mind wandering, do not worry. Acknowledge that your mind has wandered, but don't judge yourself. Be kind to yourself. Gently bring your mind back to your breathing and carry on.
- Whatever you are feeling – calm, angry, frustrated – just let it happen. Acknowledge your feelings – allowing them to be.
- Continue this for around 10 minutes – longer if you wish.
- And then, gently open your eyes.
- Now take some time for reflection. Write your thoughts in your Happiness Journal. Reflect on what you were feeling before, during and after doing this exercise.

Everyday Tasks

You can be mindful anywhere at any time. You do not need to be sitting down meditating to practise mindfulness. In fact, one of the ways to start practising mindfulness using an informal method is by incorporating it into everyday tasks. When you perform a task and are fully present as you do it, you are being mindful. You begin to train your mind to be more mindful through the day and all these small acts of mindfulness soon add up and you begin to reap the benefits.

Choose any activity you would like to do – brushing teeth, showering, making tea. Pay attention whilst you are doing the activity. Don't change how you do it – just do it as normal – but with full awareness. If you can, do the same activity for the whole week in a mindful way.

For each activity what do you notice as you perform the task? Are you more "awake" to the activity? If during the activity you find your mind wandering do not worry. Acknowledge that your mind has wandered, but don't judge yourself. Be kind to yourself. Gently bring your mind back to the activity in hand and carry on.

Brushing teeth
For example, you could try brushing your teeth mindfully every day for the week. This is what you would be looking to experience to be more aware.

- Are you fully present as you brush your teeth?
- Notice the contours of your mouth.
- How do the bristles feel against your teeth?
- What sensations are you feeling?
- Can you taste the toothpaste? What flavour is it?
- What about when you spit? How does that feel?

- What sound is the brush making against your teeth?
- How does your mouth feel when you rinse it with water?

Practise these meditations and mindfulness exercises for one week before adding Step 2 to the process.

Remember to reflect on how you feel as you do these practices in your Happiness Journal.

Step 2
Learn, Grow, Live:
Keep Learning

Learning new things is so important to your sense of happiness. There is much research to prove this and I'll go into more detail on this shortly.

I first want to tell you about my own experience of learning. Whenever I have felt really low, suffered from depression, grief or low self-esteem, one of the things that really helped me heal was learning something new. After my husband Jeremy died, I decided to embark on an End of Life Doula training course. This has enabled me to work with people who are terminally ill as they face their own mortality, and help them transition from this life into whatever is next. This gives me a great sense of purpose, and a feeling that I am really making a difference to people at a time when they are feeling scared.

On a lighter note, I also learnt to ride a motorbike; something I had always wanted to do but never had the courage to embark on. For me, this is what life is about. We learn, we grow, we live.

So, what are the benefits for bringing learning into your life?

Keeps the Brain Healthy

Just as you need to exercise to keep your muscles and cardiovascular system healthy, your brain is also kept healthy through exercise. The chemistry in your brain actually changes when you learn new things, and as the white matter (myelin) becomes denser, it becomes even easier to learn more. You are also stimulating neurons in your brain, creating more neural pathways and faster electrical pulses, which means your ability to learn faster increases.

Nurtures Relationships

Learning new things can help with nurturing new (and old) relationships. If you are attending a course you meet like-minded people who often become new friends with shared interests. Or you could take a course with your partner, children or friends and family – a great way to bond with someone.

Fights Boredom

Learning something new breaks the monotony of everyday life and prevents you getting bored. Boredom can lead to you making bad decisions.

Increases Resilience

Learning something new widens your perceptions about things and opens your mind so that it becomes easier to adapt to change. As more challenges and changes in life come your way, your resilience increases.

Helps Stave Off Dementia

Research shows that people who keep learning are less likely to develop dementia as the neural pathways continue to function.

Improves Career Prospects

Learning new work-related skills could mean you get a promotion or a pay rise as you are more competitively placed.

Opens the World Up

Learning new things helps open the world up to you as you keep up with the latest fashions and trends and it allows you to look at the world in a whole new light.

Ignites New Passions

Learning something new may just ignite a new passion in you that may invoke a new career path or vocation that you never thought would be possible.

Increases Pleasure

Learning is not a chore. In fact, it can be really enjoyable and, if creative, can give much pleasure to you and others. Learn to cook and cook for others; learn to sing and participate in a choir; learn to paint and display your artwork. Or just learn these things for the sake of learning and for your own pleasure.

Action Point

So now you know why you should Keep Learning – let's put the theory into practice. First, to calm, focus and centre you, I want you to do the Three-Minute Breathing Space (detailed below). Then, go and sit quietly for a few minutes and complete the following planning exercise. Really listen to your inner voice as you work through this task. What is going to inspire, nurture and empower you? What new learning will really rock your boat? And then, go learn!

The Three-Minute Breathing Space

So many different authors have shared this meditation in different ways but I've chosen my mindfulness teacher and trainer Shamash Alidina's version, as in his book, *Mindfulness for Dummies*, he describes this meditation really well. He suggests that this meditation acts as a bridge between formal mindfulness practice, like the Counting the Breath Meditation I taught you in Step 1, and your informal mindfulness practice when doing daily tasks such as washing the dishes or brushing your teeth. It's like checking in to your body and mind to see what's going on, what you are feeling, what you are thinking.

My routine varies so much on a day-to-day basis. I don't have a 9-5 job. One day I may be talking at a conference; the next day I may be writing an article; on another day I may be filming for my TV show; or I may be travelling for work or pleasure. So, much as I try, I am not always able to do a formal 20-30 minute seated meditation. I've stopped beating myself up over that! Instead, I've focused on this lovely Three-Minute Breathing Space – aptly named to give both my body and mind some breathing space! I'll often come out of the meditation calmer and with a clearer mind.

A couple of things to note before you get going on this. I started with this in a fairly formal way by making myself practise this meditation two to three times a day just to get into the habit of doing it. My trigger point to remind me to do it was a post-it note at the kettle – so every time I went to make a cup of tea, I performed this meditation. Once I got the hang of it, I found I was turning to it whenever I felt the need to and sometimes, time permitting, this became a five or 10-minute breathing space. Adapt it to suit your needs. We are all different, so do what works best for you.

The A, B, C of The Three-Minute Breathing Space

- Practise the steps for about one minute each.
- First start by sitting upright, (or if standing – stand tall). If you feel safe to, close your eyes.

Step A: Awareness

Bring your *awareness* to your internal experience and ask yourself the following questions:

- *What are my thoughts at the moment?*
  Acknowledge these thoughts but don't get caught up in them.
- *What emotions am I feeling at the moment?*
  Acknowledge these emotions – comfortable or uncomfortable – no need to try and change them.
- *What body sensations am I feeling at the moment?*
  How does my body feel? Am I carrying any tension or tightness in my body?
  Acknowledge these sensations – but do not try to change them – just accept them.

Step B: Breathing

- Now focus on your *breathing*.
- Take time to give attention to each breath – from the time you breathe in to the time you breathe out. Feel the rise and fall of your abdomen as you inhale and exhale.

- If you find your mind wandering do not worry. Acknowledge that your mind has wandered, but don't judge yourself. Be kind to yourself. Gently bring your mind back to your breathing and your abdomen – and carry on.

Step C: Consciously Expanding

Now take your awareness from your abdomen and *consciously expand* to the rest of your body. Be aware of your posture and your face, and feel the whole body breathing. If you feel any sensations or tensions in your body, acknowledge them but don't try and change anything – just be aware. In that moment accept what is, what your body is and what you are feeling. You are in full present moment awareness.

Take a few minutes to write down any thoughts, feelings and reflections in your Happiness Journal.

Adapted from Mindfulness for Dummies – S. Alidina[11]

Planning

Now, having done the Three-Minute Breathing Space, and without spending too much time thinking, write down 10 things that interest you.

1) _____

2) _____

3) _____

4) _____

5) _____

6) _____

7) _____

8) _____

9) _____

10) _____

Now, looking at the list, choose three things that you would perhaps like to learn more about.

1) _____

2) _____

3) _____

You could also consider learning something that you used to know and have forgotten – a language, for example.

Research and Booking

Now, do some research online to see what courses are available that align with your interests. Remember that courses may be offered online, at your local college or as part of adult services run by your local council. Look in local magazines and also speak to people. Word of mouth is sometimes the best way to hear about local courses.

Once you have found a suitable course – don't wait – go book it.

Learning can also be done from books and online talks like TEDx, but research shows that attending a course with like-minded people is more beneficial.

Step 3
The Power of Thought:
Changing Your Mindset

I was diagnosed with clinical depression in my late twenties. For me this was a huge matter of shame. The fact that I was hospitalised, couldn't hold down a job and couldn't function socially was deeply humiliating for me. I felt like I was letting down all the people in my life including my partner Jeremy, my family and my friends.

I remember thinking:
How can a strong person like me be so weak?
How can I, a confident and determined woman be
diagnosed with a mental health illness?
How will people look at me now?
Will they think I am weak and not trust me anymore?
Will I ever be taken seriously again?
I feel like I am a failure and a disappointment.
Will I ever get better?
Will I ever get over this?

For me, clinical depression was like walking with a grey, fuzzy cloud over my head all the time. Physically my body ached from the top of my head to the tips of my toes. I felt like I couldn't breathe. My stomach felt tight all the time, my heartbeat was fast and I would suffer from panic attacks. Every breath I took felt like an effort.

Being diagnosed with clinical depression made me feel like I had a weak mind and therefore I reasoned that I must be a weak person.

But, with time, medication and therapy, I learnt that in fact it was a medical condition that I needed treatment for. But, because it's not a visible condition (like a broken leg), you can't always explain it or people aren't always sympathetic because they don't understand. This was probably the first time in my adult life that I felt truly vulnerable.

But from vulnerability comes courage.

As my understanding of the illness grew, I became less worried about what people thought and began to realise that I was ill, but I could get better. This realisation was what I held on to.

As I got better and stronger over the months, and learnt more about depression and mental health illnesses, I decided to be more open about what I had gone through. I started talking and blogging about my experiences. In 2014 I became a Voice of

Mind – the leading mental health charity in the UK. I was featured in the media and in the Houses of Parliament lobbying MPs for better funding and awareness for mental health treatment. I became an accredited mindfulness teacher and started working with people who suffered from stress, depression and bereavement. I became a champion for better understanding of mental health in the UK and whilst writing this book, I am looking to raise awareness here in my home country, Kenya.

I have this burning desire to share my experience of true fear and vulnerability, from which can then come courage, empathy and positivity.

I have now developed coping skills that serve me well and these are the 10 steps I am sharing with you.

And so, step 3 is about changing your mindset.

Making the mental shift from what is wrong with our lives to what we want in our lives is often difficult. But this mental shift is an important one. It is something that we can do at any time, in any situation – it is our choice. In life there are always things that are difficult or problematic, but if we can find a way to change pain into positivity, we may just find a way to be happy!

If we look closely at our thoughts, we can see that when we focus on only the problems, we feel bad, sad, or depressed. It is harder to find a solution if we dwell on how difficult our problems are.

And so, to nurture happiness, we must develop positive mental habits and this is what this step is about.

Action Point

Mantra Meditation

Meditating using mantras is one of the most popular methods of meditation. This meditation gives me something to focus on to calm my mind.

I am a huge fan of Deepak Chopra and it was from his teachings that I learnt to meditate when I first started meditating by using mantras. Chopra suggests that when you are meditating you are tuning into your mind rather than trying to escape it.

We have around 60,000 thoughts a day. Many thoughts overlap one another – and we don't even realise we are having these thoughts. Through meditation you can slow down the number of thoughts that enter your mind, and also create a gap between each thought. Chopra explains that meditation should be a way to get into the gap between the thoughts that are floating through your head, as well as make each gap longer.

The premise is that by focusing on and repeating a mantra silently, you are able to achieve a state of inner calm and pure awareness and thus enter a deep state of meditation.

Mantra is a Sanskrit word. *Man* is mind and *Tra* is instrument. An instrument of the mind. I like that!

A popular mantra, and my favourite, is *So Hum (I Am)*. For me, repeating this allows me to just be.

Give it a try as follows:
- Sit in a comfortable position – be that on a chair or on the floor. You can lie down if you are unwell – but be aware that you may fall asleep when meditating lying down – and that is not the purpose of this meditation.
- Place your hands in your lap or on your knees with the palms open and facing the sky.
- Allow your eyes to close gently and begin to focus your attention on your breath.
- Now introduce the mantra *"So Hum"* repeating it silently.
- If you find that you are distracted by your thoughts or any noises around you, acknowledge them and gently bring your focus back to repeating the mantra.
- Breathe naturally, inhaling and exhaling with ease.
- You can decide how long you want to meditate. Perhaps start at 10 minutes and work your way up to 30 minutes every day, and then if possible, twice a day. Whatever timescale you choose, stick to it. So, if you are meditating

for 10 minutes then set the timer for 10 minutes so that you are committed to that time. Remember, don't beat yourself up if you find you have not been able to meditate for as long as you would have liked – choose one of the shorter meditations described in this book.

- When your meditation is complete, release the mantra and focus on your breath. Take a few moments to rest and then gently open your eyes.
- Take a few minutes to write down any thoughts, feelings and reflections in your Happiness Journal.

Negative Thoughts

We all sometimes have negative thoughts about ourselves. Perhaps it is about our looks or our work or our relationships. We sometimes worry about what people think about us.

Write down here any negative thoughts you might have at this moment about yourself.

For example, I might think *"I am not strong enough to do this"*.

1) _____

2) _____

3) _____

Positive Affirmations

Affirmations are short, powerful statements which you say or think and believe to be your reality. They are in effect your conscious thoughts.

We have thousands of thoughts every day. Many of these thoughts are in our subconscious. We aren't even aware that we are thinking them. And these thoughts will affect how we behave, how we react, and how we are.

Negative or critical thoughts can be seen to be our reality even when they are not. This can lead to negative implications in our mind and body. By declaring firmly and positively that something is true you can change the way your mind works. You reframe your negative thoughts with the affirmation.

Now, write a positive affirmation that will counteract each of the negative thoughts you wrote.

For example, my affirmation in response to the negative thought *"I am not strong enough to do this"* is *"I am brave"*.

1) _____

2) _____

3) _____

Now repeat the affirmations silently and firmly until you are saying them with true conviction and belief.

Step 4
The Joy of Gratitude:
Being Grateful

I love this activity because as I write it mindfully, I am doing so with gratitude in my heart. Gratitude for everything that I can enjoy in my life. Gratitude for the moment that I am in. Gratitude for enjoying life in full consciousness.

In fact, as you live more mindfully, you find that you become more grateful for what you have, rather than resentful about what you don't have. So, for example, when I am eating a plate of food mindfully, as well as experiencing, the colour, the aroma, the flavours of the food, I am acknowledging the presence of this food, and how grateful I am for this food, when so many in the world go without.

It's well documented that people who express gratitude for what they have and what they experience, feel happier. If you are feeling a little low, writing down the things you have to be grateful for is a really good exercise.

Some people write their Gratitude Journal once a day, some a few times a week and some weekly. I don't have a set time. I don't want to put myself under any pressure to achieve. I don't want it to be something else that I *have* to do. Another thing on my endless lists of things to do. Instead, I want to pick up my Gratitude Journal whenever I feel like it and write in it whenever the urge takes me. Interestingly, this act of writing has a lasting effect on me, enabling me to sleep better and feel less stressed. But, perhaps the most profound effect on me is that it is an antidote to comparing myself with others.

I am on social media a lot and most of the time it is a positive experience. But like everyone, there are times when it saps me of my energy, especially when I find that I am comparing myself to others. Seeing other people achieving more success than me, having more fun than me or being fitter than me, leads to me feeling inadequate. I ask myself why am I not as popular, successful or thin, and so the self-doubt continues! This is a destructive pattern that can really spiral out of control if you allow it to.

But, when I write down the things I am grateful for in my life, no matter how small they are, I find that I am happy with what I have. I am grateful, thankful and so very blessed. Even when things are tough, and trust me, there have been some tough times, I find that I can find something to be grateful for, and it changes my perspective on life.

As you record the things you are grateful for, you may be surprised by what is important to you. I've done this exercise with hundreds of people, and the things they write down are always the same. And it's not the car, the house, the money and so on. It's the small things that make a big difference. Sometimes it can be as simple as a cup of tea after a long day, or the warmth of sunshine after a long, dreary winter or the company and listening ear of a close friend when things are not going so well.

Take a look at the action point and begin to cultivate gratitude in your heart for all that is good in your life.

Action Point

Gratitude Meditation

- Sit quietly for a moment and bring your attention to your breath.
- Then bring your attention to your heart centre.
- Think of something that you are grateful for today – big or small - it doesn't matter.
- Write this down – mindfully and with gratitude in your heart.
- Do this again two more times.

Gratitude Journal

You can either have a Gratitude Journal in which you write once a day, a few times a week or weekly. Just do what feels right for you. Use a simple lined notebook and follow this format.

Date: _____
Today I am grateful for:

1) _____

2) _____

3) _____

Spend some time reflecting on the things you have written down.

Step 5
Compassionate Me:
Practising Compassion

What exactly is compassion?

Compassion, as defined by the *Concise Oxford Dictionary*[12], is the *"Pity inclining one to help or be merciful."*

But compassion is much more than that. It is the act of being kind, showing consideration and a spirit of generosity to all people (including yourself), animals and the environment.

As I mentioned earlier, in 2015 I was very fortunate to see the Dalai Lama speak in London. I can't explain it, but he just exuded goodness, kindness and compassion.

As he articulates so eloquently in his book *How To Be Compassionate*[13]:

"In order to achieve peace, tranquility, and real friendship, we must minimize anger and cultivate kindness and a warm heart. As we become nicer human beings, our neighbours, friends, parents, spouses, and children will experience less anger, prompting them to become more warm-hearted, compassionate, and harmonious. The very atmosphere becomes happier,

which even promotes good health. This is the way to change the world."

So that's what this step is about – compassion.

But first, compassion must start with the self. Self-compassion, self-care.

Some people see this as selfish and I completely disagree. You know how in an aeroplane safety briefing they always say in the case of an emergency put the oxygen mask on yourself first then help the person next to you? That's how I see life. How are you able to give to others and be compassionate to others when you aren't okay yourself?

So, start with some self-compassion – I have given you some ideas in your action point.

Then, look at how you can show compassion, through random acts of kindness, to others, your friends and family and perhaps even strangers.

And then finally, how can you be more compassionate to nature? Perhaps by recycling more, or volunteering at an animal shelter or simply changing your shampoo to an eco-friendly one.

Again, I have given you some ideas in your action point. So, go take a look and remember compassion is the way to change the world for the better. Now who can argue with that?

Action Point

Metta Meditation

Metta means loving-kindness and in this meditation we will be cultivating loving-kindness and compassion. It's a powerful and very moving meditation. I absolutely love it and I hope you will too.

- Ensure that you are sitting in a correct posture.
- Close your eyes. Just sit with that for a moment.
- Now bring your attention to your breath. Exhale and inhale through your nose in your own time.
- Bring your palms together and press the knuckles of your thumbs into your sternum. (There is a notch between your left and right ribcage at the level of your heart). Bring your focus to your thumbs and focus on the feeling of your heartbeat. Stay with this for a few minutes.
- Place your right palm in the centre of your chest and your left hand on top of your right hand. Feel the energy and warmth at the centre of your chest where your heart chakra is. Visualise this energy as an emerald green light.

- Visualise this green light radiating throughout your body.
- Take your awareness now to the top of the head where you have your crown chakra. Visualise a soft, white ball of light above your head, gently radiating light into your crown chakra.
- Visualise this white light radiating throughout your body.
- Now feel love, compassion and gratitude for yourself. You may find this difficult to begin with, but overtime self-compassion will get easier.
- Quietly say the words:
  "May I be happy"
  "May I be peaceful"
  "May I be free from suffering"
  "May I be happy"
- Repeat the words as many times as you wish.
- If you need to visualise the faces of loved ones or happy occasions to get that feeling of love and compassion in your mind, then do so.
- Now turn your palms outwards and away from your body.
- Visualise a mixture of emerald green energy and the bright white energy gently flowing in front of you out of your palms.

- First, imagine your nearest and dearest, the people that you most love, in front of you. Allow the energy to flow from your palms to your loved ones.
- Say the words:
  "May you be happy"
  "May you be peaceful"
  "May you be free from suffering"
  "May you be happy"
- Now imagine friends and family in front of you. Allow the energy to flow from your palms to them.
- Say the words:
  "May you be happy"
  "May you be peaceful"
  "May you be free from suffering"
  "May you be happy"
- Now imagine work colleagues and acquaintances in front of you. Allow the energy to flow from your palms to them.
- Say the words:
  "May you be happy"
  "May you be peaceful"
  "May you be free from suffering"
  "May you be happy"
- Now imagine someone to whom you may feel negativity, perhaps anger, hurt, jealousy, animosity – even if very slight – in front of you.

Allow the energy to flow from your palms to them.

- Say the words:
  "May you be happy"
  "May you be peaceful"
  "May you be free from suffering"
  "May you be happy"
- Now imagine a small globe, the whole earth in front of you. Allow the energy to flow from your palms and envelope the whole globe.
- Say the words:
  "May all beings have happiness"
  "May all beings be free from attachment and hatred"
  "May all beings be peaceful"
  "May all beings be free from suffering"
  "May all beings be happy"
- Now turn your palms to face the floor, down to Mother Earth.
- Visualise the excess energy in your body flowing down to Mother Earth.
- Silently say the words:
  "Thank you, Mother Earth, for supporting me, sustaining me and nourishing me."
- Place your hands back down on your lap with your palms open.

- Place your feet firmly on the ground and imagine roots growing from the soles of your feet down into the ground.
- Say the words silently:
  "Thank you, Mother Earth, please bless me and allow me to ground myself to you."
- Sit with your eyes closed for as long as you like.
- In your own time, open your eyes, stand up and take a few minutes to walk and stretch.
- Now take some time for some reflection and write your thoughts in your Happiness Journal. Reflect on what you were feeling before, during and after doing this meditation.

Please Note!
- Energetically speaking, this is a very strong meditation. If at any time you feel dizzy, spaced-out or faint, please open your eyes and ground yourself by stamping your feet lightly on the floor and drinking some water.
- Throughout this meditation be positive and open to any emotions, thoughts and sensations that may arise. Observe them, but do not get caught up in them. Allow them to be.
- If you need to stop for any reason, then go back to your breath to calm your mind and body.

- If you have high blood pressure, are pregnant or unwell, then approach this meditation gently.

Practising Compassion

Below are suggestions to help you start practising self-compassion, compassion for others and for nature this week.

Remember, these are only suggestions – do what's right for you and as many or as few as you like – and be as creative as you want with your activities.

Self-Compassion

"A moment of self-compassion can change your entire day. A string of such moments can change the course of your life."

Christopher K. Germer[14]

Here are some suggestions to enable you to cultivate self-compassion.
- Book an aromatherapy massage.
- Take 15 minutes to write a list of your good traits/achievements you are proud of – and put them in a prominent place where you can see them.
- Put aside a little time every day this week to do something special for yourself. You could meditate, read a book, take a walk, watch TV

– whatever you consider relaxing and nourishing for your mind, body and spirit.
- Bake a cake. Eat cake!
- Spend time in nature – go for a walk, go to the beach.
- Connect with a loved one or a close friend. Enjoy a coffee, talk, laugh, cry!
- Spend time journaling or filling in a gratitude diary.

Write some of your own suggestions here:
- _____
- _____
- _____

Compassion to Others

"Whether one believes in a religion or not, and whether one believes in rebirth or not, there isn't anyone who doesn't appreciate kindness and compassion."

Dalai Lama[15]

Here are some suggestions to enable you to show compassion to others.
- Hug someone.
- Send someone flowers for no reason at all – just to make them smile

- Do a chore for someone. Something you know they don't particularly enjoy doing like cleaning the bathroom!
- Invite a friend or family member to join you in one of your meditations, perhaps the Metta Meditation.
- Pop a card in the post to let a friend know you're thinking about them.
- Stop your car to let people cross the road – be safe!

Write some of your own suggestions here:

- _____
- _____
- _____

Compassion to Nature
"Water and sun green these plants. When the rain of compassion falls, even a desert becomes an immense, green ocean."

Thich Nhat Hanh[16]

Here are some suggestions to enable you to show compassion to nature.
- Walk or cycle somewhere instead of jumping into the car.
- Donate money to a wildlife or nature charity.

- Make sure you are recycling everything that is recyclable.
- Have a shower instead of a bath. Make it a short shower!
- Use organic, natural cleaning products for the house that are kinder to the planet.
- Buy locally-sourced fruit and vegetables.
- Do a short meditation focusing on the earth and all the living creatures.

Write some of your own suggestions here:

- _____
- _____
- _____

Step 6
Nourish the Body:
Getting Active

It's really simple – we are holistic beings!

If the body and the mind and the spirit are not in alignment – if even one of the three aspects is out of sorts – then we will not feel whole. We will not have complete wellbeing.

And that is why the 10 techniques in this book are so powerful. They work on the mind, the body and the spirit to bring wellbeing to each one of the three elements so that we have complete wellbeing.

In this chapter, we look at physical wellbeing, specifically nourishing the body with exercise.

Exercise can mean so many different things to every one of us. For some people the thought of going to the gym fills them with dread, whilst for some people a week without regular visits to the gym feels like something is missing. Attending a dance class might be unthinkable for some and yet for others, missing their weekly dance class means that they are out of sorts for the rest of the week. It's just wonderful that we are so different and that we can all turn to different activities - dance, yoga, sports, gardening, walking the dog, even housework - to keep us fit, healthy and happy.

Yes happy, because as well as feeling fit and probably looking great, physical activity releases the chemical dopamine into our system.

Dopamine is a chemical found naturally in the human body. It is a neurotransmitter, meaning it sends signals from the body to the brain.

Dopamine plays a part in controlling the movements a person makes, as well as their emotional responses. The right balance of dopamine is vital for both physical and mental wellbeing.

Dopamine deficiency can have a significant impact on a person's quality of life, affecting them both physically and mentally. Many mental health disorders are linked to low levels of dopamine.

As I mentioned earlier, we are integrated holistic beings, and so our physical wellbeing affects our mental wellbeing, which affects our spiritual wellbeing, which affects our physical wellbeing. And so, the cycle, or the relationship between the three elements, continues.

Take a look at the action point and this week make sure you schedule in some physical exercise. Stick to something you are used to or try something new. Do what works for you.

The meditation for this step is a body scan. I have chosen this because having an awareness of your body in this space and time is very powerful. It is extremely centering and mindful and it teaches you to accept your body in that moment.

Have a lovely time getting active and benefitting from the positive cycle that results from exercise. And the main thing is – have fun!

Action Point

Body Scan

The body scan is a very popular mindfulness technique and involves bringing awareness to the various parts of the body, step by step.

For many, this may be a difficult exercise, keeping one's attention focused on one part of the body for any length of time, but do stick with the practice of this as it really does help develop concentration and calmness and overall mindfulness.

The aim of the body scan is not necessarily relaxation, although you may find that you do relax as a result of this process. Rather, the aim is to experience your body as it is. To bring full awareness to the sensations within your body, experiencing and acknowledging the sensations you are feeling, without any judgement, but rather with a sense of gentleness and curiosity.

The body scan is normally done lying down – allowing your body to be fully supported by the floor or bed that you are lying on. If you find yourself falling asleep you may want to do the body scan seated or even with your eyes open. Do what works for you.

Ensure that you have a quiet space, with no interruptions. It must be a place where you will feel safe and comfortable. Allow anything from 30 to 60 minutes for this exercise. Keep a blanket with you in case you get cold.

Firstly, remove your shoes and loosen any clothes that may feel tight.

Lie on your back on a mat on the floor or on your bed, arms by your sides, legs can be straight or bent at the knees. Remember do whatever is comfortable for you.

Allow your eyes to close gently.

Let the mat or bed support your weight. Notice where your body makes contact with the mat or the bed and with each breath allow yourself to sink deeper into the supporting surface.

Bring your awareness to your breath, breathe naturally and acknowledge the rise and fall of your abdomen. Stay with this for a few minutes.

If at any time you find your mind wandering, do not worry. Acknowledge that your mind has wandered, but don't judge yourself. Be kind to yourself. Gently bring your mind back to your body and carry on.

Toes, Feet and Legs

- Take your awareness to the big toe on your left foot. Notice any sensation you may be feeling. Acknowledge the sensation, and then move on to the next toe. As you go from toe to toe acknowledge the different sensations – the warmth, the cold, the tingling, no sensation at all.
- Breathe into your toes – imagining your breath travelling from your nose all the way down to your toes! And then breathe out.
- Now take your awareness to the sole of your left foot – the ball of your foot, the arch, the heel. Acknowledge the sensations. Breathe into the sole of your foot. Take the awareness to the top of the foot, feeling the sensations there and in your ankle. Breathe into the whole foot and then release.
- Now, using the same method slowly work up the leg, to the shin, calf, knee and thigh. At each point bring awareness to the body part, acknowledge any sensations and then breathe into that body part.
- Practise the same thing on your right side – toes, sole, heel, ankle, shin, calf, knee and

thigh. At each point bring awareness to the body part, acknowledge any sensations and then breathe into that body part.

Pelvic Area, Lower Abdomen, Lower Back

- Take your awareness to your pelvic area. Notice any sensation you may be feeling. Acknowledge the sensation.
- Breathe into your pelvic area.
- Now, using the same method slowly work up to the lower abdomen, round to your buttocks and to your lower back. At each point bring awareness to the body part, acknowledge any sensations and then breathe into that body part.

Chest, Upper Back, Shoulders

- Take your awareness to your chest. Notice any sensation you may be feeling. Acknowledge the sensation.
- Breathe into your chest area.
- Now, using the same method slowly work round to your middle back, upper back and shoulders. At each point bring awareness to the body part, acknowledge any sensations and then breathe into your back.

Fingers, Hands and Arms

- Take your awareness to your left hand. Notice any sensations you may be feeling in your fingers. Acknowledge the sensation, and then move on to the next finger. As you go from finger to finger acknowledge the different sensations – the warmth, the cold, the tingling, no sensation at all.
- Breathe into your fingers.
- Now take your awareness to the palm of your left hand – and then into the top of the hand and wrist. Acknowledge the sensations. Breathe into the whole hand and then release.
- Now, using the same method slowly work up the arm - to the forearm, elbow, upper arm and to the shoulder. At each point bring awareness to the body part, acknowledge any sensations and then breathe into that body part.
- Practise the same thing on right arm. At each point bring awareness to the body part, acknowledge any sensations and then breathe into that body part.

Neck, Head, Face

- Take your awareness to your neck. Notice any sensations you may be feeling.

Acknowledge the sensation and then move on to the jaw and chin.

- Now, using the same method slowly work up your face, your lips, your mouth, your tongue, your cheeks, your nose, your eyes and eyelids, your ears, your temples, forehead, the top of your head and then finally the back of your head. At each point bring awareness to the body part, acknowledge any sensations and then breathe into that body part.

Bring your attention back to your breath. Breathe from the top of your head all the way to the tips of your toes. Keeping your awareness on your breathing get a sense of the whole body being still and calm. Breathe naturally as you rest in this moment of pure awareness.

Take a few minutes to write down any thoughts, feelings and reflections in your Happiness Journal.

*Adapted from The Mindful Way Through Depression: Freeing Yourself From Chronic Unhappiness –
M.Williams, J. Teasdale, Z. Segal, J. Kabat-Zinn[17]*

Physical Wellbeing

What are your goals for your physical wellbeing?

For one person it may be progression to the next level of fitness, whereas for another it may be maintaining a level of fitness.

For one person it may be to maintain a healthy weight, whereas someone else may want to lose weight, and another may want to gain weight.

You need to decide for yourself what your physical fitness goal will be to suit your body and lifestyle and fit in with your other goals.

My physical fitness goals are: _____

_____

_____

_____

_____

_____

_____

_____

_____

_____

_____

_____

What exercise or physical activity do I need to do to achieve my physical wellbeing?

List here what activity you would like to do and how many times a week. Also note what aspect of your physical wellbeing this is achieving e.g. cardiovascular, muscle strengthening or balance.

- _____
  _____
- _____
  _____
- _____
  _____

What obstacles may arise that prevent you from taking part in your chosen physical activity?

Despite our best intentions we may find obstacles in our way, preventing us from taking part in the exercise of our choice.

See if you can pre-empt any issues arising and how you would deal with them so that they don't interfere with your plans.

List the potential obstacles here and solutions to overcoming them.

- _____
  _____

- _____
  _____
- _____
  _____

Step 7
Power Your Presence:
Be Seen, Be Heard

- I choose to Show Up when it matters.
- I choose to always Speak My Truth.
- I choose to Stand in My Power.

Living by these three decrees means that I am seen and I am heard when it matters.

This isn't always easy. We have so many hang ups. So many things that give us anxiety, self-doubt or imposter syndrome. Sometimes I feel that we alone put these obstacles in our path and so we choose not to be seen or to be heard. And there are times when you do need to withdraw from the world. Times when you need to go inwards and reflect. Times for introspection and consolidation. There's nothing wrong with that.

But, when you don't allow yourself to be seen or to be heard, especially when you want to be, then you are doing yourself a disservice.

Being seen and being heard does not mean shouting from the rooftops, *"Look at me, listen to me, I am here"*.

Rather, being seen and being heard means having the confidence to be present, to be authentic and to have true connection with others.

And you can only do that when you choose to show up, when you harness the internal power that you have and when you choose to authentically speak your truth.

For me to be able to do these three things I have to be aligned in my body, my mind and my spirit. So, in fact, the way to be confident in these three things is first to be confident in myself. If I know that my mind is strong, if I know that my body is strong, if I know that my spirit is strong, only then will the true me be seen and be heard.

So, I have to work on these three aspects – my mind, body and spirit. Thankfully, this book has the proven techniques to help me do just that. And in a way, all the steps lead to this particular step.

I would like to look in more detail at *presence* and what that actually means.

Presence is you being present. But it is a lot more than that. It is about the positive energy that you exude in any situation. This energy comes from an internal confidence but also from your external appearance. If you feel intrinsically good and you feel good about your appearance, this will automatically help you in your presence.

When you harness this presence, or channel it in the right way, you feel empowered to make a difference to your own life and to the lives of others. When you own your presence, and you understand what enhances it, then you can use it to show up, stand in your power and speak your truth.

It's a cycle. The more I power my presence, the more I show up, stand in my power, speak my truth, which then enhances my presence, which then... and so on. You get it!

So, we have to work on our presence.

And in this step I want you to approach this by working on a couple of elements as well as defining what your presence is to you.

My presence is the knowledge that I want to live life fully, compassionately and make a difference – no matter how small. I want to do that through my work, by speaking my truth.

Remember that you owe it to yourself to Show Up, Stand in Your Power and Speak Your Truth – do not be afraid to Be Seen and to Be Heard.

Action Point

Power Your Presence Meditation

- Find a comfortable seated position and close your eyes or lower your gaze.
- Bring your focus to your breathing. Breath in through your nose and out through your nose. Honour each breath into your body and each breath out of your body.
- If you find your mind has wandered, that's okay – don't beat yourself up about it. That's what minds do. Acknowledge that your mind has wandered and then bring it back to your breathing.
- Now – say the words:

  "I choose to power my presence"
  "I choose to be seen"
  "I choose to be heard"

  "I choose to show up when it matters"
  "I choose to stand in my power"
  "I choose to always speak my truth"

  "I choose to power my presence"
  "I choose to be seen"
  "I choose to be heard"

- Take your mind to a time in your life, either professionally or personally, when you have felt happy and in control. A time when you have felt like you have been seen and you have been heard. Take your time.

- Now you have that memory in the forefront of your mind, remember the feeling it gave you. How did you feel knowing that you were being seen and being heard? Focus on that positive feeling.
- Next imagine a situation in life in which you would like to be seen and to be heard. This may not have happened yet. Imagine it happening.
- Harness that positive feeling you had from your memory and imagine that you are having these positive feelings for this new situation that you wish to happen.
- You feel happy, you feel positive. You feel seen. You feel heard. You are confident and self-aware and empowered.
- Now – say the words:

"I choose to power my presence"
"I choose to be seen"
"I choose to be heard"

"I choose to show up when it matters"
"I choose to stand in my power"
"I choose to always speak my truth"

"I choose to power my presence"

"I choose to be seen"
"I choose to be heard"

- Stay with that for a moment and then slowly allow yourself to come back to the room. Stand up and stamp your feet on the ground gently and drink some water to ground yourself.
- Take a few minutes to write down any thoughts, feelings and reflections in your Happiness Journal.

Define Your Presence

What does presence mean to you? Write down what you think your presence is. It may be that you don't think you have the presence yet. If that is the case, write down what you would like your presence to be. Defining your presence gives you the confidence to work towards embodying it and harnessing its power.

My presence is: _____

_____

_____

_____

_____

_____

_____

List Your Goals

Listing your goals, whether personal or professional, will clarify what you want from life. Knowing what you want, focusing on achieving what you want, making connections and being confident and authentically present means that you are powering your presence!

- _____
  _____
- _____
  _____
- _____
  _____

Identify Your Style

Your personal style needs to give you confidence, make you feel positive and empowered. Do not dress for others. Dress for yourself.

Looking at your external appearance, what is your personal style?

My personal style is:

_____
_____
_____
_____
_____

I am happy with my personal style because:

_____

_____

_____

_____

_____

I want to make the following changes in my personal style:

_____

_____

_____

_____

_____

Strong in Mind
I feel strong in my mind because:

_____

_____

_____

_____

_____

_____

Strong in Body
I feel strong in my body because:

_____

_____

_____

_____

_____

_____

Strong in Spirit
I feel strong in my spirit because:

_____

_____

_____

_____

_____

_____

Step 8
The Art of Giving:
Giving to Others

As a species, we are hardwired to be altruistic. That bond that we form with another when we do something for them with no expectation of a reward, is reward in itself and no monetary value can be put on that.

Whether it be giving our time or money or expertise, it doesn't matter. It is the act of giving that matters.

Volunteering has been shown to increase good health and happiness and improves life satisfaction.

When my husband died, I realised that I should look outwardly to others who needed my help. It was important for me to feel that I was making a difference in his name. I think I also needed to channel my grief in a positive way.

So, in January 2017, I set up the Jeremy Lucas Education Fund (JLEF) under my sister's lion conservation project – Ewaso Lions.

"Educating youth, empowering communities, encouraging conservation" is the fund's strapline and

it is now in its fourth year, and is going from strength to strength.

JLEF currently supports 16 young people in secondary and tertiary education in Samburu northern Kenya. For these young people, affording further education and all the associated costs would be impossible. The continued support that JLEF will give them until they secure jobs means that they are looking towards positive, bright futures where they can look forward to successful careers in their chosen fields.

I see each and every one of these young people as my children. I worry about them, I get nervous when their exam results are due and I feel pure happiness when they do well in school or college. I know that Jeremy looks over them and gives them his blessing too.

But from a purely selfish point of view, helping these young people makes me full good. It makes me feel like I am making a difference. It makes me happy to see them happy and flourishing. It gives me strength.

And that's what giving does. We give for unselfish reasons and yet we benefit when others benefit.

So, in this step I want you to think about how you want to give to others. And by that I don't just mean a monetary donation through an online website. Take the time to really think how you are going to give back to society, to the human race, to our earth, to animals. Whatever it may be and whether that be through fundraising, volunteering or raising awareness for a particular cause, choose something to focus on. I urge you to do this because once you start looking outwardly and seeing how you can give to others, how you can be altruistic, then your life really will change. It's so powerful.

I want to share this lovely quote by the Dalai Lama[18] which says, *"This is my simple religion. No need for temples. No need for complicated philosophy. Your own mind, your own heart is the temple; the philosophy is simple kindness."*

Action Point

Giving Meditation

"You give but little when you give of your possessions. It is when you give of yourself that you truly give."

Kahlil Gibran[19]

Giving your time, your skills and your attention is often the best gift that you can give.

- Close your eyes and bring your attention to your breath, inhaling and exhaling gently through your nose in your own time.
- Now allow your mind to go to a moment when someone has given you something in a time of need. Perhaps they have helped you when you have been ill, or done you a favour when you were desperate or just listened to you when you needed to unburden yourself. Allow yourself to go back to that time and remember how it felt to be supported.
- Now focus on how your body is feeling as you remember that situation. What emotions are you feeling right now? Rest in that feeling for a few moments. Take your attention to your heart centre and see how you are feeling. Is your heart open to receiving?

- Now, with your mind and heart open to receiving, take your attention to an instance when you have given someone your time or your skills or your attention with no expectation of remuneration. And your gift was gratefully received. How does your body feel now? What emotions are you experiencing? Rest in this moment with these feelings for a while.
- Take your attention to your heart centre and see how you are feeling. Is your heart open to giving?
- Sit with that for a moment, bring your attention back to your breath and then when you are ready slowly open your eyes.
- Take a few minutes to write down any thoughts, feelings and reflections in your Happiness Journal.

List of Causes

Write a list of causes that you are interested in or passionate about. Perhaps it is raising funds for a certain disease; or raising awareness about a certain cause; or working at an animal shelter. Don't think too much – just brainstorm and write from the heart.

- _____

_____

- _____
  _____
- _____
  _____
- _____
  _____
- _____
  _____
- _____
  _____
- _____
  _____

One Cause

From the list above, narrow it down to one cause that you are particularly passionate about.

The cause I am most passionate about is:

_____
_____

I am passionate about this cause because:

_____
_____
_____
_____
_____

Method of Giving Back

Write three ways that you would like to give back to this particular cause – perhaps raising funds, raising awareness, volunteering. Be specific on how you will achieve these aims.

- _____
  _____
  _____
  _____
  _____

- _____
  _____
  _____
  _____
  _____

- _____
  _____
  _____
  _____
  _____

Now you have decided what cause you want to give back to, and how you are going to do that, go forth and give. There is nothing stopping you. Good luck!

Step 9
Connection:
Building Relationships

Humans are social beings. Yes, there are introverts and loners who prefer their own company and we all need the solitude that gives us a chance to recharge, but over all we need social interaction to survive and to thrive. Connection is key for us.

Whether it be conversations with friends, community life, a dance class, a religious festival, a family sharing Sunday lunch or just two people having a drink together, our aim is to interact with others, be aware of each other, sharing emotions and common interests.

We live in a fast-paced, consumer-driven society and through technology we are more connected to each other than at any time in history. On social media we share more than we have ever shared before, measuring success, and therefore happiness, by our status, our achievements and the things we accumulate.

We judge our connection to people by the number of followers we have on Facebook, likes on our Instagram posts, retweets on Twitter and comments on our blogposts. Our smartphones and laptops ping constantly hailing the arrival of a WhatsApp message or email. Yes, we are more connected than ever before, and yet, the reality is that we have never felt more disconnected and alone.

The irony is that all our social media presence is geared to showing how not alone we are, how we are enjoying life with friends and family, and just how happy we are, and yet social isolation is growing at an alarming rate in our societies.

Once seen as an affliction of only the elderly, loneliness is now an epidemic among young adults.

It is important to distinguish between solitude and loneliness. Solitude is an important part of our self-care. Being alone once in a while to refresh oneself is important, as long as it is in the context of a healthy social life. But, when that solitude is actually day after day of being isolated, then it turns into loneliness.

I've written quite a lot about loneliness because when Jeremy died, I really understood true loneliness. The type of loneliness that is crippling in its strength. Loneliness that saps you of the energy and the will to live; loneliness that is frightening and debilitating in its relentlessness; loneliness that can kill.

It should be said that one can feel lonely in the company of others too, especially in toxic or unhappy relationships. Loneliness can hit you when you are surrounded by people whose lives seem to be moving forward whilst yours is at a standstill.

I recently read somewhere that Britain is the loneliness capital of Europe, and research shows that loneliness can be twice as deadly as obesity. And so, for consolation and company we turn to social media, television, alcohol, medication and food.

The truth is that we are not designed to cope alone. Without real human connection we will wither.

And the relentless online digital connection that we engage in does not give us the social intimacy required to really nurture lasting relationships, form bonds or feel true human connection.

It would be unrealistic to say give up social media completely – although periodic social media detoxes are highly recommended. Instead, it's important to use the time spent online in a more productive way, harnessing the power of social media connection to enhance and not detract from true human connection.

After all, authentic, real and personal connections we form with the people we encounter, even in brief encounters, can be truly magical.

Action Point

Mindfulness of Breath

Building on from the One-Minute Mindful Breathing Meditation and the Three-Minute Breathing Space, this lovely, simple meditation really grounds and focuses me. Seated meditations can be done sat on a chair or on the floor. Find a comfortable position that works for you and allows you to be grounded, stable and sitting with your back straight and dignified.

If you are seated on a chair, make sure you are seated upright with your feet flat on the ground. You may need to sit forward in your chair. If you have any back pain then do support your back with cushions or the back of the chair. Place your hands lightly in your lap, palms facing up. Your spine should be in neutral, with your body aligned and sitting on your sitting bones. Ensure your neck and head are not jutting out but in alignment with the rest of your spine.

If seated on the floor use a mat. You can kneel, supporting your buttocks with a meditation stool or cushion or you can sit on some cushions to support your buttocks with your feet crossed in half lotus with your knees supported on the floor. Your hips need to be higher than your knees. Place your hands lightly in your lap, palms facing up. Ensure your neck and head are not jutting out but in alignment with the rest of your spine.

- Close your eyes if you feel comfortable to do so. Just sit with that for a moment.
- Now bring your attention to your breath. Exhale and inhale through your nose in your own time.
- Feel the different sensations as you breathe in and out – the breath on your upper lip, the rise and fall of your chest and stomach.
- Keep your attention on your breath.
- If you find your mind wandering, do not worry. Acknowledge that your mind has wandered, but don't judge yourself. Be kind to yourself. Gently bring your mind back to your breathing – and carry on.
- Whatever you are feeling – calm, angry, frustrated – just let it happen. Acknowledge your feelings – allowing them to be.
- Continue this for around 10 minutes – longer if you wish.
- And then, gently open your eyes.
- Now take some time for reflection. Write your thoughts in your Happiness Journal. Reflect on

what you were feeling before, during and after doing this exercise.

Adapted from Mindfulness for Dummies – S. Alidina[20]

Finding and Nurturing Relationships

Who we choose to spend our time with says a lot about our mental and spiritual happiness. How we nurture our relationships shows how joyful or not we are feeling inside.

What does a good relationship mean to you?

_____

_____

_____

_____

_____

List all the positive relationships in your life.

- _____

_____

- _____

_____

- _____

_____

- _____

_____

- _____

_____

- _____
  _____

Pick three of the most important relationships from the list above and for each of them write three things you will do for each person that will nurture your relationship and show the person that you love them.

- _____
  _____
  _____
  _____

- _____
  _____
  _____
  _____

- _____
  _____
  _____
  _____

List any toxic relationships that you have in your life.

- _____
  _____
- _____
  _____
- _____
  _____

For each of those toxic relationships, how are you going to change or end the relationship?

- _____
  _____
  _____
  _____
- _____
  _____
  _____
  _____
- _____
  _____
  _____
  _____

List the type of relationships you are looking to add to your life.

- _____
  _____
- _____
  _____
- _____
  _____

For each of those relationships, write down how and where you might be able to find these like-minded people – and then action those points.

- _____
  _____
  _____
  _____
  _____
- _____
  _____
  _____
  _____
  _____
- _____
  _____
  _____
  _____
  _____

Remember that your time is precious and you should it spend it as much as possible with people who enhance your physical, mental and spiritual wellbeing. If a person is draining your emotional energy, then that relationship is not serving you well. When looking at the various relationships in your life, ask yourself if spending time with the person is making you feel uplifted, supported, inspired or listened to. Are they interested in you, are you interested in them? Are you able to hold clear boundaries with the people in question? Is the relationship mutually kind and loving?

When you are happy and content and have a sense of wellbeing, you are vibrating at a higher level which means you attract people who match your vibration. In turn you give back to them the best version of yourself.

Be clear about what it is you are looking for in all your relationships with friends and family. Then, work towards nurturing those relationships accordingly.

Step 10
Nourishing the Body:
Eating Well

Mindful Eating

I used to suffer a lot from stomach ailments – cramps, bloating, upset tummy. And, despite numerous medical tests nothing was found to be wrong in my stomach. The doctor suggested that it was probably stress related and that I may be allergic to certain foods. This was not good news, as I had never been allergic to any foods before. She also told me to cut out spicy foods. Oh my! She had no idea who she was talking to! I love my curries and Tabasco sauce on everything.

I did make some changes but they were half-hearted and I never really got better!

Until I started practising mindfulness and meditation daily. Within weeks I saw a difference. It wasn't so much about *what* I was eating but more about *why* and *how* I was eating.

Firstly, just the fact that I was meditating calmed my mind and had beneficial physiological benefits on my body. I was now able to handle stress better and generally had a more positive outlook to life.

When I got angry or upset, I was able to acknowledge the emotions and deal with them in a positive way. This made me a mentally and physically healthier person.

Also, it has made me a lot more aware of what I eat. Eating mindfully meant I paid more attention to how the food looked and tasted. I found I also needed a lot less to feel full and satisfied.

The old me:
When I was stressed, angry, upset or depressed I would reach for crisps or sausage rolls to give me that salty kick, or cakes and chocolate if I wanted something sweet. I frequently missed breakfast, and if I did eat it, it would be sugary cereal or toast with margarine and jam. Lunch was often a cheese toasty and dinner would be pies, chips, takeaway Indian curries and Chinese food (laden with MSG) and a lot of red meat – beef steaks, lamb steaks and pork sausages. At every meal I would add extra salt to my food and wash this down with a couple of glasses of wine every night. I would justify this consumption of fatty, unhealthy foods by saying that I was eating low-fat yoghurts and drinking skimmed milk. My intake of fruit and vegetables was also very low. I would rather reach for a

chocolate bar than for an apple. I ate a lot of bread and huge amounts of pasta.

So, as you can see, it was not a healthy diet. Being unaware of my emotions was leading me to make bad food choices. Both my body and mind were suffering.

The new me:
Pay attention to what I eat. Look at the food, smell the food, taste the food with full present moment awareness. If something does not look appetising, e.g. a sausage roll with fatty, soggy pastry and pink, synthetic looking meat in it, I don't eat it. If the chocolate bar smells overly sweet and sickly, I don't eat it. If I put a crisp in my mouth and all I can taste is salt and the oiliness of the crisp, I don't eat it. I pay attention to my mood. What emotional state am I in? Am I hungry or am I angry? Am I hungry or am I bored? Am I hungry or am I stressed? Chances are that I may be feeling more stressed, angry or bored than hungry. Once I have identified the real emotion, I can deal with it appropriately.

That's it! I did lots of practical things and I've listed them here. But, it's not just about the practical solutions. It's about changing your mindset and your emotional response to food. Once I had that sorted, I was able to take practical steps to change what I ate, how I ate it and when I ate it.

- Don't keep crisps, chocolates and other unhealthy snacks in the house. Instead have a go-to box for healthy snacks such as nuts or dried fruits. If you are eating crisps and chocolates, do so mindfully.
- Always have a bowl of fresh fruit at hand and aim to eat one piece of fruit every day. I love grapefruit in the morning and an apple in the evening. I will also always eat a banana before I teach a Just Jhoom! dance class.
- Have more vegetables than meat on a plate – I always make sure that any meat is the smallest thing on my plate.
- Don't eat any processed food with ingredients that you can't pronounce! If I don't know what it is, I'm not eating it.
- When you buy fruit and vegetables, make sure they are fresh – look at them, feel them, smell them.
- Choose colourful foods. This really changed the way I ate. If it is white or brown and has no colour or vibrancy then chances are it doesn't taste good and isn't healthy. Fresh fruit and vegetables come in a variety of

colours so make sure you eat what is pleasing to the eye.

- Variety is key! I have a rule – put something new in my shopping basket whenever I go shopping. A fruit or vegetable I have not tried before, a packet of lentils or beans that I don't know how to cook – but hey I'll learn!
- Eat slowly and mindfully. Don't eat with the TV on, or at your desk at work. Stop doing everything else and take time to eat. Savour each mouthful before you take another bite. If you are sharing food with friends and family, don't eat unconsciously as you carry on the conversation. To eat in silence and appreciate your food is not a bad thing!

Using all these tips, plan to eat your next meal mindfully.

Mindful Cooking

Cooking can be a real chore. Especially if, like me, you don't particularly like cooking. I always saw it as a waste of time. But we need to eat. And, as much as I hate cooking, I love eating. Food was such an important part of my life growing up. In fact, my family made a living from food. My father owned a hugely popular chain of Indian Mughlai restaurants in Kenya and my mother is an exceptional cook.

Today, I am quite fussy with what I eat. I am not keen on fast food, take-away meals and ready-made meals. I like my food to be freshly prepared with good, fresh, locally-sourced ingredients.

So, I decided that I needed to change my attitude towards the whole activity of cooking. Instead of cooking whilst watching TV or half-heartedly cooking whilst I thought about work and the one million things I needed to do, I decided to make cooking a mindful activity.

I would source good ingredients, spend time planning the dishes, follow a recipe and create a satisfying meal.

One of my oldest and dearest friends, Cheeku, loves to cook and create new recipes. She put a creative and innovative collection of healthy Indian recipes into a Just Jhoom! book - *Cook to Jhoom!*

These recipes are tried and tested and turn typical Indian dishes into healthy, contemporary creations, suitable for busy people to cook, and make healthy choices.

In this step I want you to explore both the aspects of mindful eating and mindful cooking. For both these you will need to set aside some time. If cooking or eating with family members, tell them what you are doing and perhaps include them in the practice. Try the Raisin Meditation with them. It always evokes a multitude of reactions!

Action Point

Mindful Eating – Raisin Meditation

The aim is to eat the raisin mindfully, paying attention to everything you are doing, moment by moment, and appreciate the full experience of eating the raisin.

You will probably spend about 15-20 seconds on each of the following stages of the activity. Do not rush. Take your time.

- **Hold**

First hold the raisin between your thumb and fingers. Feel the texture and the weight of it in your hands. Take a moment to think about the journey this raisin has made to get to you. Where was it grown? Where was it dried? How was it transported to you?

- **Look**

Now look at the raisin – the size, shape, colour – notice any markings on it. Imagine that this is the first raisin you have ever seen.

- **Listen**

Rub the raisin between your fingers. Does it make any sound as you do this?

- **Smell**

Smell the raisin. Does it have a scent? What does it smell like? Does your body react in any way to the scent?

- **Put in Mouth**

Put the raisin in your mouth. Notice your hand and arm movements that enable you to do this. Notice how your tongue reacts to the raisin being put into your mouth. Allow the raisin to roll around your mouth. How does this feel? What is its texture?

- **Chew**

Now bite into the raisin. What sensations do you feel? What does it taste like?

- **Swallow**

Let the raisin go down your throat. What does that feel like? Can you sense it going down to your stomach? How many times do you have to swallow until the raisin is all gone? What does your mouth feel and taste like when the raisin is all swallowed? Is there an aftertaste?

- **Reflect**

Write your thoughts down in your Happiness Journal. What did you feel before, during and after doing this exercise? Did you have any thoughts relating to other foods; your like or dislike of raisins?

How did your body react to eating the raisin? Were you salivating as you anticipated eating? Did your stomach rumble? Did you want another one, or was this one raisin enough?

Adapted from Mindfulness for Dummies – S. Alidina[21]

Mindful Cooking

I've chosen one of my favourite dishes to share with you. Aubergine is such an under-rated vegetable, and yet cooked well it can be delicious, not to mention very versatile. This is a very simple recipe – even I can make it!

Take your time cooking this, doing everything mindfully and focus on the act of cooking.

Aubergine Fiesta

Serves 4 as a main, 6 as a side dish
Preparation time: 15 minutes
Cooking time: 30-35 minutes

"This recipe has been inspired by two of my favourite dishes: an Indonesian dish called Terong Balado which consists of fried aubergines served with a garlicky tomato-chilli sauce or sambal and the Egyptian dish Kosheri (thank you Yottam Ottolenghi for your excellent recipe) which includes a tangy and hot tomato sauce married with cinnamon-flavoured rice, vermicelli, and lentils. I combined some of these flavours with Indian flavours to create this delicious grilled aubergine dish.

Beware, it is quite hot! You can use milder chillies and deseed them, but if you can handle the heat, then this is the dish for you. Do try and source the pomegranate seeds for this recipe – they add a sweet balance to these hot, tangy and slightly smoky aubergines."

Cheeku Bhasin – Author of *Cook To Jhoom!*[22]

<u>Ingredients</u>
- 2 medium aubergines (about 500g total), sliced into 5mm roundels along their length
- 600g chopped tomatoes (skins removed, canned are fine)
- 100g fresh pomegranate seeds
- 4 cloves garlic (12g), minced
- 3 small red chillies, finely chopped (use less and deseed, if you prefer) or you can use larger, milder chillies
- 2 tablespoons cider vinegar
- 1½ teaspoons cumin powder
- ¾ teaspoon cinnamon powder
- Sea salt to taste
- 3 tablespoons (12g) finely chopped fresh coriander
- 400ml water
- 2 tablespoons + 1 teaspoon sunflower/olive oil

Method

Start by making the tomato sauce. Heat 1 teaspoon of oil in a pan on medium heat, fry the minced garlic until lightly coloured. Add the chopped tomatoes, chillies, vinegar, cumin and coriander powders and salt. Stir for a minute or two before adding the water. Reduce the heat to a simmer and let the sauce cook down for 30-35 minutes. Taste and adjust seasoning. This should be quite a thick sauce and taste tangy and hot. Remember that you will be adding pomegranate seeds for sweetness, so don't add any sugar.

While the sauce is cooking, heat a griddle pan on low-medium heat, brush the aubergine slices with oil and grill slowly on the pan, seasoning them as you do. You want to do this slowly, turning them from time to time so that the aubergines cook and get the chargrilled flavour. They should be light brown and soft when they are done. This will take about 12-15 minutes per batch. Another way to do this is to put the oiled and seasoned aubergine slices under a low-medium heat grill, turning them once. Because the slices are thin, this should take about 15-20 minutes.

When the sauce and aubergines are done, layer the aubergine slices on a serving platter, top with the tomato sauce, fresh coriander and pomegranate seeds – or you can mix it all together - and then arrange and serve. As a main course, this dish is wonderful with steamed rice!

There are so many other simple yet delicious recipes you can try from *Cook To Jhoom!*

My favourites include: Steamed Masala Fish with Fennel, Spicy Roasted Cauliflower and Mari Chicken Wings.

Available to buy from www.justjhoom.co.uk

Mindful Eating
Firstly, write down your feelings about food. Discuss your relationship with food. Is it a normal relationship that you are happy with, or do you have some food issues? Why do you think this is?

Secondly, prepare a meal mindfully.

Thirdly, serve the food and then enjoy a mindful meal. Take time to savour each bite. What tastes good? What does each dish taste of? What about the textures of the food in your mouth? What does that feel like?

Take your time with each mouthful. No rush. Make sure you swallow each mouthful of food before you take another one.

At the end of the meal, take a few minutes to write your reactions down in your Happiness Journal. What did it feel like having to swallow each mouthful before taking another? What did the textures of the food feel like? Were you able to eat everything on your plate? Did you eat more or less than normal? Did you have an adverse reaction to any food?

It has been shown that people who adopt mindful eating habits make better and healthier food choices. So, turn the TV off, sit at your dining table and give the food in front of you the attention it deserves. Smell the food, look at the food, taste the food, and savour and relish every mouthful! Eating well will help you stay mentally well. So, be mindful of what you put into your body, showing it that you love it and want to nourish it.

I want to end this chapter with a short story of how I came to mindfulness in the first place – and it has to do with masala chai! Some of you may have read this in my memoir *Always With You*.[23]

When I suffered from depression in my late 20s, I started doing a very simple, non-taxing job in a local arts centre in the Surrey village that I lived in. It was perfect – photocopying flyers and posters and putting them up on noticeboards or around the centre was just about all I could manage.

I'd return home at midday, utterly exhausted, and make myself a cup of *masala chai*, the old-fashioned Indian way; the way my mum used to make it. First, I'd boil some water in a saucepan, then slowly I'd add the spices, then the black tea leaves and finally the milk and sugar, until it all bubbled up into a fragrant mix. I'd perform each step deliberately and carefully, paying close attention to the simmering water, to my stirring and to the wonderfully warm, pungent aromas of cinnamon, cardamom and fennel seeds that wafted up from the saucepan. I found it calming, meditative even, so different from the way I did things in the past. Before falling ill, I was a bundle of energy, always rushing around, performing a hundred different tasks at once: putting on the lunch; taking out the washing; opening the post; all the while talking on the phone or to Jeremy. But I was incapable of functioning like that anymore. My brain was so befuddled that all I could do was focus on one task at a time. And making *masala chai*, I found, relaxed me; it slowed me down.

Once it was made, I'd sit in the conservatory, taking long, slow sips from the hot mug clasped in my hands, allowing the warm tea to soothe me.

This was my first (unintentional) introduction to mindfulness. And, I have never looked back. As a result, I chose to study to become an accredited mindfulness and meditation teacher and have now taught the practices to hundreds of people around the world, both face-to-face and through my online courses. Mindfulness changed my life and I am grateful I have been able to share this practice with so many people in the last few years.

Conclusion

In the nine months that I have taken to write this book, my life has changed completely.

After my husband, Jeremy, passed away in July 2016 the grief was paralysing in its intensity but as the grief lifted and the desire to become happy took over, I began to implement the 10 steps that I have shared with you in this book. But that does not mean that the work is done. Each of these steps has given me the strength and courage to move forward. As I became more resilient, I realised that I could not go back to my old life because without Jeremy my old life was non-existent. To truly move forward, I had to make a completely new life for myself – make new memories, in new places, with new people.

Although it wasn't a decision I took lightly, once I took it, I felt a sense of freedom and excitement, as well as an innate knowledge that this was right for me.

The idea was to set off for the biggest adventure of my life!

And so, in the summer of 2019 I got rid of most of my worldly belongings, rented out my house and left the Surrey village that I had called home for 19 years – with plans to travel the world for three years.

I started off by staying with a cousin in London for a few months. I realised that I wanted to experience London life, as well as honouring some work commitments I still had in England. During that time, I did a Jhooming Farewell Tour around the UK, visiting some key instructors and teaching Just Jhoom! in various locations; I ran my last Just Jhoom! class in Cranleigh and said goodbye to my friends and dance students with a fantastic, bittersweet farewell party; I took a holiday to Sri Lanka where I drove a tuk-tuk around the island for two weeks; I experienced London with all its hype, buzz and excitement.

I'm now in Kenya, where I had planned to be for only a few months before I travelled to Italy to work on a vineyard in Tuscany. But things haven't quite turned out as I planned.

I have now decided to stay in Kenya for the foreseeable, as I embark on a new career, reconnect with friends and family, and rediscover the place of my birth. So many exciting and unexpected things are happening right now – that it seems that this is the place to be. And so, I choose to remain here for as long as it feels right to do so. If things change, I will move on. Also, I am lucky that I have my small cabin in Nanyuki, at the foot of Mount Kenya, on land that was bought by Jeremy. It is where I feel closest to him and at my most peaceful – and so I visit it often.

It's funny, but I was a real control freak as a young child. And I took that into my adult life. I wanted to control everything from my work, to my body, to my relationships. When Jeremy died, I realised just how little control I really have. Yes, we have free will, and we have the right to make choices, as we should. But making choices is very different to trying to control everything.

I believe you should make good choices that are beneficial to you, and then you release those intentions to the universe and allow it to do its magic.

Yes, make plans – it would be foolish not to. But, don't stick to them too rigidly; be flexible. Also, give yourself time and space to just be, to wait and to listen to what the universe is saying and where it is inviting you to go. Because when you listen, and are truly present, the universe will gift you in ways that you could never imagine. It will create opportunities that you never even dreamed of. It will open doors that you didn't even know existed.

Because the universe works in mysterious and magical ways. All we need to do is have an open mind and open heart and we will hear it.

So, as you embody the 10 steps in this book, I ask you to do so with an open mind and an open heart.

Continue to practise the meditations that you have learnt, to journal your thoughts and feelings, to practise the steps as feels right for you. And whilst you are working through my 10-step programme, show yourself compassion. Be kind to yourself, because it won't always be easy.

And remember, life is hard… but it is also beautiful.

You will fall, but you will rise again.
You will fail but you will learn from that failure.
You will cry, but you will laugh too.
You will love, and you will grow, and you will live.

Because this is life… hard but also beautiful.

Change your mindset and you will cultivate happiness, compassion and resilience from within.

And I promise that you will live a more joyful, meaningful and mindful life. This is my hope and prayer for you.

Free Online Resources

Please visit:
https://www.justjhoom.co.uk/happiness-free-resources/

Or scan the QR code below.

Contact Shalini Bhalla-Lucas

Join me on Facebook   @justjhoom
Follow me on Instagram   @justjhoom
Watch me on YouTube   /JustJhoom
Visit my website   www.justjhoom.co.uk

And read The Jhooming Nomad blog
www.thejhoomingnomad.blog
to see where in the world I am and what I am up to!

Further Reading

I have listed all the books I have read or used for reference over the years. This information is for reference only – we are all different and what works for me may not work for you.

Happiness

Bloom, William. *The Endorphin Effect*. London: Piatkus Books, 2001

Dolan, Paul. *Happiness by Design*. UK: Penguin Random House, 2014

His Holiness the Dalai Lama and Cutler, Howard C. *The Art of Happiness: A Handbook for Living*. London: Hodder and Stoughton, 1998

Narain, Nadia and Narain Phillips, Katia. *Self-care for the Real World*. UK: Penguin Random House, 2017

Unger, Arlene K. *How To be Content: An inspired guide to happiness*. London: White Lion Publishing, 2018

Woollard, William. *Buddhism and the Science of Happiness*. UK: Grosvenor House Publishing, 2010

Spiritual Awareness

His Holiness the Dalai Lama. *How To Be Compassionate: A Handbook for Creating Inner Peace and a Happier World*. UK: Rider, 2011

Gilbert, Paul. *The Compassionate Mind*. London: Constable, 2009, 2010, 2013

Kornfield, Jack. *Bringing Home the Dharma: Awakening Right Where You Are*. Boston: Shambhala Publications Ltd, 2011

Morley, Charlie. *Lucid Dreaming: A Beginner's Guide to Becoming Conscious in Your Dreams*. London, Hay House UK Ltd, 2015

Rinpoche, Sogyal. *The Tibetan Book of Living & Dying*. UK: Rider, 2008

Tolle, Eckhart. *A New Earth: Create a Better Life*. London: Penguin Books, 2005, 2006

Mindfulness and Meditation

Alidina, Shamash. *Mindfulness For Dummies*. West Sussex: John Wiley & Sons Ltd, 2010.

Hanh, Thich Nhat. *Peace Is Every Step: The Path of Mindfulness in Everyday Life*. London: Rider, 1991

Hart, William. *The Art of Living: Vipassana Meditation*. India: Embassy Book Distributors, 1987

Kabat-Zinn, Jon. *Full Catastrophe Living: How to cope with stress, pain and illness using mindfulness meditation*. London: Piatkus, 1990, 2013

Williams, Mark and Penman, Danny. *Mindfulness – A Practical Guide to Finding Peace in a Frantic World*. London: Piatkus, 2011

Quote Credits

Every effort has been made to correctly credit the quote sources, but if any have been inadvertently overlooked or incorrectly referenced, please contact the publishers.

[1]Woollard, William. *Buddhism and the Science of Happiness*. UK: Grosvenor House Publishing, 2010 (Pg ix)

[2]Aristotle Quotes. BrainyQuote.com, BrainyMedia Inc, 2019. https://www.brainyquote.com/quotes/aristotle_138768 (Online - accessed 27 January 2020)

[3]Preston, Douglas. *I Took The Dalai Lama To A Ski Resort And He Told Me The Meaning Of Life*. www.businessinsider.com/i-took-the-dalai-lama-to-a-ski-resort-and-he-told-me-the-meaning-of-life-2014-11?IR=T, 2014 (Online - accessed 27 January 2020)

[4]Lesarge, Lmakiya. *Proverbs of the Samburu*. Kenya: Aura Publishers, 2018 (Pg 226)

[5]Dolan, Paul. *Happiness by Design*. UK: Penguin Random House, 2014 (Pg 3)

[6]Thompson, Della (Editor). *The Concise Oxford Dictionary*, *Ninth Edition*. UK: Oxford University Press, 1996 (Pg 1171)

[7]Williams, Mark and Teasdale, John and Segal, Zindel and Kabat-Zinn, Jon. *The Mindful Way Through Depression: Freeing Yourself from Chronic Unhappiness*. New York: Guilford Press, 2007 (Pg 21-22)

[8]His Holiness the Dalai Lama. Dalai Lama Quotes. BrainyQuote.com, BrainyMedia Inc, 2020.

https://www.brainyquote.com/quotes/dalai_lama_166116
(Online - accessed 27 January 2020)

[9]Williams, Mark and Teasdale, John and Segal, Zindel and Kabat-Zinn, Jon. *The Mindful Way Through Depression: Freeing Yourself from Chronic Unhappiness.* New York: Guilford Press, 2007 (Pg 47)

[10]Williams, Mark and Penman, Danny. *Mindfulness – A Practical Guide to Finding Peace in a Frantic World.* London: Piatkus, 2011 (Pg 4)

[11]Alidina, Shamash. *Mindfulness For Dummies.* West Sussex: John Wiley & Sons Ltd, 2010. (Pg 115)

[12]Thompson, Della (Editor). *The Concise Oxford Dictionary, Ninth Edition.* UK: Oxford University Press, 1996 (Pg 270)

[13]His Holiness the Dalai Lama. *How To Be Compassionate: A Handbook For Creating Inner Peace and A Happier World.* UK: Rider, 2011 (Pg 5)

[14]Germer, Christopher K. *The Mindful Path to Self-Compassion: Freeing Yourself from Destructive Thoughts and Emotions.* New York: Guilford Press, 2009 (Pg 2)

[15]Dalai Lama Quotes. BrainyQuote.com, BrainyMedia Inc, 2020. https://www.brainyquote.com/quotes/dalai_lama_132541
(Online - accessed 27 January 2020)

[16]Hanh, Thich Nhat. *Present Moment, Wonderful Moment: Mindfulness Verses for Daily Living.* USA: Rider 1993 (Pg 94)

[17]Williams, Mark and Teasdale, John and Segal, Zindel and Kabat-Zinn, Jon. *The Mindful Way Through Depression: Freeing Yourself from Chronic Unhappiness.* New York: Guilford Press, 2007 (Pg 104-106)

[18]His Holiness the Dalai Lama. *How To Be Compassionate: A Handbook for Creating Inner Peace and a Happier World.* UK: Rider, 2011 (Pg 120)

[19]Khalil Gibran Quotes. BrainyQuote.com, BrainyMedia Inc, 2020. https://www.brainyquote.com/quotes/khalil_gibran_105674 (Online - accessed 27 January 2020)

[20]Alidina, Shamash. *Mindfulness For Dummies.* West Sussex: John Wiley & Sons Ltd, 2010. (Pg 101)

[21]Alidina, Shamash. *Mindfulness For Dummies.* West Sussex: John Wiley & Sons Ltd, 2010. (Pg 86)

[22]Bhasin, Cheeku. *Cook to Jhoom!* USA: AuthorHouse, 2012 (Pg 20)

[23]Bhalla-Lucas, Shalini. *Always With You – A True Story of Love, Loss…and Hope.* UK: Just Jhoom! Ltd, 2018 (Pg 77)

Photo and Design Credits

Cover Design by Angela Basker

<u>Front Cover:</u>
Shalini's Photograph © 2018, Sian T. Photography
www.siantphoto.com (Instagram: @siantphoto)

<u>Back Cover:</u>
Shalini's Photograph © 2019, Sian T. Photography
Author Photograph © 2018, Sian T. Photography

A Word of Thanks...

My sister Shivani, for showing me that we can think outside the box, achieve the impossible and be anything we want to be.

Mum for being the strong woman that she is, and instilling the confidence and belief in both my sister and I that we can be equally strong, if not stronger.

Mom – Ushamasi – for having true belief in me and everything I do, for being another strong and inspiring woman in my life, and for welcoming me into her home with open arms.

Pinky Lilani for her support over the years – and for the foreword to this book.

Sian T, for her continuing friendship, wonderful photography skills, and all the publicity and portrait photographs.

Angela B, for her friendship, excellent design skills and designing this book cover.

Clare D for editing and proofreading and seeing all the mistakes I didn't see!

My London family for giving me a roof over my head when I had none and making me feel so welcome – Bharat D, SheruM, KalpanaM.

Amar V for finally reading between the lines... and bringing fun and laughter into my life.

And to you the reader – thank you for buying my books and continuing to support me. I am forever grateful.

About the Author

Shalini Bhalla-Lucas is an award-winning author, entrepreneur, TV presenter, motivational speaker, trainer and the founder of **Just Jhoom!** She is also an accredited mindfulness and meditation teacher – teaching highly-effective, proven techniques to help combat stress, anxiety and depression.

Shalini has performed all over the world and has had TV appearances on **BBC, ITV, Channel 4** as well as on numerous radio stations and podcasts. She has been featured in publications such as the **HuffPost,** *RED* **magazine and** *Top Sante,* discussing physical, mental and spiritual wellbeing through dance and mindfulness.

She was chosen to be one of 10 people in the UK to be a voice of the mental health charity **MIND** – campaigning for better mental health provision, addressing MPs in the UK Houses of Parliament.

In 2010 Shalini set up **Just Jhoom! and created the world's first accredited Bollywood dance-fitness instructor training programme** – training over 300 instructors worldwide, releasing a dance-fitness DVD and CD, a healthy-eating Indian cookbook and a children's illustrated book.

In 2013 Shalini won the **Asian Women of Achievement Awards in Arts and Culture** and was also named as *"One of 20 Female Entrepreneurs Energising Britain"* by *Real Business*. In January 2012, she won **the Surrey Advertiser Business Accelerator Award**. She was featured in **Who's Who of Britain's Business Leaders 2009 - 2011**. In January 2016, Just Jhoom! was a finalist at the **Cranleigh & District Business, Innovation & Growth (BIG) Awards.**

In January 2017, Shalini set up the **Jeremy Lucas Education Fund** in Kenya in memory of her beautiful, kind husband, Jeremy Lucas, who passed away in 2016 after a two-year battle with cancer.

She is a trained **End of Life Doula and Pranic Healer** working with terminally-ill cancer patients.

Shalini self-published her memoir *"Always With You – A true story of love, loss...and hope"* in July 2018 which became a No 1 Amazon Bestseller three months later.

"Online Dating @ 40 – The Nobheads, Nutjobs & Nice Guys" Shalini's second book, is a funny and candid account of the highs and lows of online dating and was published in February 2019.

In May 2019, Shalini was one of six women from the UK to be featured in **TRESemmé's Power Your Presence** Online

Masterclass, alongside celebrities Emma Willis, Alesha Dixon and Christine Lampard.

In 2019, Shalini wrote regular columns in two UK magazines as well as numerous guest blogs and her own two blogs – **Just Jhoom!** **www.justjhoom.co.uk/blog/** and **The Jhooming Nomad** www.thejhoomingnomad.blog

In March 2020, Shalini's third book *"Happiness! Is It Simply A Mindset Shift?"* was officially launched in Kenya as well as world-wide on Amazon.

Shalini's passion is in promoting physical, mental and spiritual happiness and health through her writing, speaking, teaching and media work. She is also an avid women's activist – specifically raising awareness of the plight of widows around the world.

Always With You

A true story of love, loss...and hope.
By Shalini Bhalla-Lucas

At 21, Shalini Bhalla knew where she was heading in life.

Born into a successful Indian family in Kenya, Shalini – at university in England – was preparing to one day take over the family business. Everything was mapped out... until she met and fell in love with her English neighbour, Jeremy. Then her world turned upside down.

For the first time in her life she found herself at odds with her parents and was faced with an agonising choice: to follow her heart or to submit to her parents' wishes.

Shalini's decision would take her on an extraordinary journey of self-discovery – one that took in family estrangement, severe depression, spiritual and physical renewal, devastating loss and, finally, hope.

Always With You is the gripping and inspiring story of one woman who found the strength and courage to carve out her own path...

Above all it is a testament to the power of love.

Available from www.justjhoom.co.uk or Amazon

Printed in Great Britain
by Amazon

39582571R00095